Waldrep's seventh collection begins where his prior collection, *feast gently*, left off: "This / is how the witness ends: touch, withdraw; touch again," according to the opening poem in *The Earliest Witnesses*. If these are poems of witness, then they are also testators to the craft of seeing: eye-proofs of an epiphenomenal world. "Can you see *this*," the ophthalmologist in "A Mystic's Guide to Arches" asks over and over again. Sight becomes both the facilitator and impediment of desire, in collusion with language itself. "She said, When you say *pear*, I see *p-e-a-r* for a second before I see, in my mind's eye, a pear," Waldrep carefully records in "[West Stow Orchard Poem (II)]." The desire-poems in *The Earliest Witnesses* want the thing itself, its image of the mind, and the language that transmutes both thing and image into song.

"There is no poet today or in days past who writes like G.C. Waldrep. His voice, his insight, and his vivid lyricism are one-of-a-kind. His diction is startling, unerringly musical. I want to befriend this voice and listen to all it says about the confounding strangeness of being alive on this planet. This book possesses Waldrep's characteristic spirituality and keenly seeing eye, but these poems show a new vulnerability, a wrestling with mortality and the ubiquity of war ('Tell me more about your childhood, the war murmurs, trying to place its mutilated / hand on mine'). The poems of *The Earliest Witnesses* are indelibly contemporary even as they reach beyond into centuries to come. They thrum with high-voltage intelligence and a palpable love of nature as they confront human violence and suffering. Waldrep is a visionary poet." —Rachel Galvin

"*The Earliest Witnesses* suggests the dividing line between the mortal and the eternal is not death, but the body, and an insoluble problem troubles this nexus insofar as the body is occupied by thinking—it recognizes the difficulty of simultaneously standing both in and beside the world, but, remarkably, it recognizes also that fully inhabiting this difficulty is the beginning of peace: 'For we too know wheels, & are known of them. / ... Alongside some music we had made. Or just after.' This is beautifully intelligent, beautifully achieved poetry." —Shane McCrae.

"I have been an avid reader of G.C. Waldrep through seven collections and nearly twenty years. *The Earliest Witnesses* puts in stark relief the way his lightning mind, caught between God and the body, finds in poetry the battery to hold and express the voltage. As always, his linguistic palette and image-making are electric. What is new? The poems here are more naked and more fierce; in them I feel the charge of crisis: of faith and of earth, psyche and flesh. 'I have a fever and its name is God,' he writes. I walk with him." —Dana Levin

THE EARLIEST WITNESSES

G.C. WALDREP is the author most recently of the collection *feast gently* (Tupelo, 2018), winner of the 2019 William Carlos Williams Award from the Poetry Society of America, and a long poem, *Testament* (BOA Editions, 2015). Waldrep's poems have appeared in *Poetry, Ploughshares, APR, Paris Review, New England Review, New American Writing, Harper's, Tin House, Conjunctions*, and many other journals in the USA and abroad, as well as in the *Best American Poetry* anthology series and the second edition of Norton's *Postmodern American Poetry*. With Ilya Kaminsky he co-edited *Homage to Paul Celan* (Marick, 2011) and with Joshua Corey he co-edited *The Arcadia Project: North American Postmodern Pastoral* (Ahsahta, 2012). Waldrep's work has received prizes from the Poetry Society of America and the Academy of American Poets as well as the Colorado Prize, the Dorset Prize, the Campbell Corner Prize, two Pushcart Prizes, a Gertrude Stein Award for Innovative American Writing, and a 2007 National Endowment for the Arts Fellowship in Literature. He lives in Lewisburg, Pa., where he teaches at Bucknell University and edits the journal *West Branch*. From 2007 to 2018 he served as Editor-at-Large for *The Kenyon Review*.

THE

EARLIEST

WITNESSES

G.C. Waldrep

TUPELO PRESS
NORTH ADAMS, MASSACHUSETTS

Tupelo Press
PO Box 1767
North Adams, Massachusetts 01247
(413) 664-9611 / Fax: (413)-664-9711
editor@tupelopress.org / www.tupelopress.org

Also published in Great Britain by Carcanet
Alliance House, 30 Cross Street
Manchester M2 7AQ, U.K.
www.carcanet.co.uk

Book design by Andrew Latimer

Tupelo Press is an award-winning independent literary press that publishes fine fiction, non-fiction, and poetry in books that are a joy to hold as well as read. Tupelo Press is a registered 501(c)(3) non-profit organization, and we rely on public support to carry out our mission of publishing extraordinary work that may be outside the realm of the large commercial publishers. Financial donations are welcome and are tax deductible.

CONTENTS

American Goshawk	3
Caynham Camp	6
I Have a Fever and Its Name Is God	9
A Mystic's Guide to Arches	11
Croyland Abbey	14
Mutter Museum with Owl	16
Native, Like a Quince	19
North Walsham	21
Broken Things	24
Never-Ending Bells	25
Shall Bear Upon His Shoulder in the Twilight	27
On the Feast of the Holy Infants Killed for Christ's Sake in Bethlehem	28
In Him Were Hidden All Our Tongues	29
Blue Heron, Marlborough	32
Jones Mountain Eclogue	35
The Constellations	36
On Being Mistaken for "Part of the Art" at the Mattress Factory Museum in Pittsburgh	39
Only Coerce Yourself Gently, & Show	42
(Wordwell I)	44
(Wordwell II)	46
(Wordwell III)	48
On Hearing a Cuckoo at Pentecost	50
Pentecost, Risby	51
[West Stow Orchard (I)]	52
[West Stow Orchard (II)]	54
Denizen (West Stow Orchard)	56
[West Stow Orchard (III)]	57
[West Stow Orchard (IV)]	59
[West Stow Orchard (V)]	60

To the Bank Holiday Caravans in Eastnor Park 61

[St Melangell's Day, Eastnor (I)] 62

[St Melangell's Day, Eastnor (II)] 63

[Ely Cathedral] 64

[St Melangell's Day, Eastnor (III)] 66

[St Melangell's Day, Eastnor (IV)] 68

[St Melangell's Day, Eastnor (V)] 69

[St Melangell's Day, Eastnor (VI)] 71

Hephaestus in Norfolk 72

[Additional Eastnor Poem (I)] 74

[Additional Eastnor Poem (II)] 76

[Additional Eastnor Poem (III)] 77

[Additional Eastnor Poem (IV)] 80

[Additional Eastnor Poem (V)] 82

[Additional Eastnor Poem (VI)] 84

[Additional Eastnor Poem (VII)] 86

[Additional Eastnor Poem (VIII)] 88

[Additional Eastnor Poem (IX)] 90

[Additional Eastnor Poem (X)] 92

Hansen's Disease 93

After the Abolition of Festivals 94

The Earliest Witnesses 95

[The Line, Its Sleek Ark. Stow] 97

[Llandyfeisant Church (I)] 98

Castle Woods, Dinefwr 99

[Dinefwr Castle (II)] 101

[Dryslwyn] 102

[Llandeilo Churchyard (I)] 104

[Llandeilo Churchyard (II)] 107

[Carn Goch] 109

[Carreglwyd) 112

[Llandyfeisant Church (II)] 113

Notes on Poems 117

Acknowledgments 121

THE EARLIEST WITNESSES

AMERICAN GOSHAWK

I strode into the woods in a brute faith, certain the forest
would give me what I needed. If there was a mathematics
I was all for it, math being hunger's distaff cousin.
This was after the season of the yellow ladyslipper,
these woods' lone orchid, though I saw their green tread
everywhere, bipedal among the needles and hush.
I was no longer in love with my life, or with anyone's.

I was thinking of Bulgakov's Ivan, stumbling around
Moscow in his night clothes with a paper icon
pinned to his chest—and who in the end must promise
to give up the practice of poetry (*bad* poetry)
in order to achieve something like peace. I asked myself
just what are you trying to see *through* (remember,
Jesus ate and drank with his disciples, to prove

that He was not a ghost). It was the strongest hour
of the day. I could feel my vows being lifted from my body
the way a novice cook lifts a heavy pot lid, carefully
and with more than the usual fear. At the Fire Pond
I paused and waited. I could see what I had come for
on the opposite side; it was intent; it was hunting.
It is very easy to be forgotten outside of one's own time.

It is very difficult to be forgotten within it. The problem
is that I am not able to respond as you demand—
and you, it seems, are not able to respond as I demand,
or would demand. And so we wound one another.
Meanwhile the season stretched into its various clocks.
Meanwhile in a whirl of blood and recognition
time began to pass again. We circled one another,

we made noises at one another as animals do
when they impede in one or more of the six dimensions.
The land beyond the pond had been logged
and I lost the path in the refuse, the clotting punk.
New ferns were hemming the mulch, seedling maples
for whom any brief interruption in the light
is that and only that. I had a stick I brandished, a stout

length of windfall oak I'd broken from the wreckage.
Either you looked edible or you seemed a credible
threat, I'd told the painter a few nights before,
her trauma multiplying across that gentle evening meal.
We think if we know the words for things we might
converse with them, we might render the world's mirror
a translucency. Behind that mirror is hunger's wall

and behind hunger the electrons go zinging as per laws
that inscribe the names of God on the natural
weft. St Paulinus of Nola: "Fire will be the judge
and will rush through every deed." He tended the bones
of the saint he felt had succored him. Yesterday
I sang the hymns of the fathers, and tomorrow
I will sing among the people for whom singing satisfies.

I told my friend, "Choice is the difference between
man and God." And the state is at its most monstrous
in this cycle. "And the angel bathing in some
piano / Turns around again wrapped in sound / Looking
for the receiver in the peaks" (Huidobro,
by way of Weinberger). I admit I enjoyed my bellowing
and brandishing. I admit I thought I could lose an eye

(if not a tooth). This is perhaps as good a way as any
to state my fear: that I will never in this body
be naked again, that I will always be naked so long
as I am in this body. We made an appointment
and we kept it, but I bear no record in the flesh. The eye's
meat is considered a delicacy in some cultures. This
is how the witness ends: touch, withdraw; touch again.

CAYNHAM CAMP

(1)

Through curtains, winter light. Late Mandelstam
open on the table. "Exile" means we are still in this life,
we are still in love with this life
where a fleet steams by in midnight Latin, new ghosts
for whom the heart crochets a new song. It's their birthday
and, like children, they know it. Like children
they capture insects to pull off their wings,
tie threads to the fragile legs of honeybees and wasps.
It is cold where the children are, but so brightly lit.
I read Mandelstam in the morning. I am not abandoned.
At the supermarket it's all I can do
to point to the meat I want, pink jewel in its crystal case.

(2)

I photographed the hollies by the inturned gate,
something regal, or as if the hill had developed lips, as if
the summit were working slowly
back towards a capacity for speech. My own tongue
a debt in it, a stud. I had barely spoken to anyone
in weeks, nodding to the waiter
at the dim French restaurant as if I were a foreigner.
I took a wrong turn in the medieval quarter
and found myself part of a procession, dark-clad, silent.
It was an accident, I wanted to say,
only to remember that once again I'd been cast
in the thief's role, which is why from every
house we passed I recognized an ancient, accusing glare.

(3)

The district opened on a grid of broken stone
punctuated by pasture; the larger mammals
shifted randomly, with the gentle Brownian motion
of hunger that has not yet reached despair, cannot imagine
that with some slight displacement of the body
every desire won't be met.
Then they were all around me, an encircling gravity.
I bowed, as only one fairly caught
in trespass may bow. I recognized the incised
language on the sentry trunks
and copied it carefully into the flesh of my retinas
so that I could teach it to the offending light, which buzzed
drunkenly against my shins, my temples, my chest.

(4)

And then, as if in some half-forgotten children's tale,
I found myself an inheritor
of a tiny kingdom, misted with marsh gas
and briar's rank exhaust, depleted of its saints.
The people who lived there used the wounds of red grapes
as their currency. I met a few of them;
they made a small living as pipefitters, and they professed
never to have heard of me, or where I lived.
They claimed that if you dug under the ground
you'd find no evidence at all of any prior human settlement.

(5)

They trapped songbirds and sold them on the open market.
They gave nothing as alms. I liked a few of them,
mostly the women. Perhaps the problem
was that I did not, as I'd been taught, exit as I'd entered.
Now the season touches me
in a way that feels both more distant and less hindered,
days laundered not in war but in rumors
of war's creche, past and future. For days I slide letters
unopened across my kitchen table; when I finally
do open them I don't read them, merely leave each folded
like a quiet hand in the matte lap of its torn envelope.

In the rose I waited for the sermon to break,
the last book close. I held a petal to the surface of my eye.

I HAVE A FEVER AND ITS NAME IS GOD

I have a fever and its name is God.
The nurses come in shifts
and worship it.

All around me the land suffers
from the loss of love's handkerchief.
Children sing brackish rhymes
in the lowest schools.

There is no key, only
the locked door
projected onto the city wall.
In my dreams I run from it.

The nurses bandage my body
in mathematical problems
I can't solve. I tell them
no, no, measure me
by the sweetness of honey—

Hush, they whisper.
Our names, too, are written
in the Book of the Smallest Moon.
You were brought here
in the traitors' black ambulance.
Your brother is a scar.

The nurses place bowls of fruit
around my prone body,
as sacrifices. *Not to you,*
they explain,
but to the heat you bear.

Finally I stumble
through the image of the door
in broad daylight. No one stops me.
I am prescient as a lilac.

But the nurses say
We will never leave you.
They have prepared a feast,
they have sewn my wedding garment.
There are so many of them,
far too many to count.
Each of them lifts a piece of me
to her mouth—

By the sweetness of honey.
Let me and my works be undone.

A MYSTIC'S GUIDE TO ARCHES

Utter and the land a scrap, a cusp, the crupped haunch
    that moves ahead of the carriage in its plush mechanicals.
        I apologized for my eye, my ear, my lame cartography.
Illness makes the body legible, most often to strangers.
    In a pinch the artery reverses. Pleasure is not an arch
through which the body passes, as from one element
    to another, *here* versus *there,* the spin of particles
        in their constituent, mutually-convoked sockets,
which scientists say is one of the few qualities of matter
    that can survive a black hole. I arrived into dead spots
in my vision, little brass keys where no locks had been
    and all around the desert's terrible graffiti. Can you see
        this, the ophthalmologist asked, from the depths
of her phone: can you see *this.* When the one-legged
    bird settled in my quince I watched to see whether
its nest would differ in any material, discernible way
    from other nests, but I had no other nests for comparison,
        only drawings in a guidebook, blurred snapshots
from the internet. It laid two eggs, one of which
    I found broken, vacant at the field's gapped edge. Wide
channels in the karst *communicate.* "As when two people
    are reading the same page, each is aware of the other's
        breath, so shall I draw in the breath of his longings,"
wrote not Gertrude (the Great) of Helfta but Gertrude's
    anonymous chronicler. The nuns of Helfta were trained
in the trivium and the quadrivium and Gertrude
    had been a child oblate. In my dream my own children
        read an article about the water armonica, filled all
the kitchen glasses from the tap, then beat them down
    into damp sand, singing loudly. I cut my feet on the shards.

It was my first dream in weeks, months perhaps,
　　　the drugs having resolved briefly into their animal clefs.
　　　　I keep scanning for entrances and exits. But I fled
the desert, which like any altar went right on cataloguing
　　　its faiths and husks. The wisteria in the arbor was not
yet blooming. I saw the feather on the forest path
　　　but would not pick it up. Nations passed through nations.
　　　　　The order of one lost feather versus the order of more
than one, the nonce court of hunger so pure, so *now*
　　　all flight reclines before it. The depression at the center
of each red blood cell is blind, the way breathing
　　　is blind. Through the glass roundel representing the sun
　　　　and then the one representing the moon, somehow
aloft again above the donor rebus. On the island, later,
　　　the orchard remnants seemed to gesture towards
where I lay, a petition. Bone is the same everywhere,
　　　you scoffed, but that isn't true. Hugh of Balma noted
　　　　"In a strict sense, to seek by night can mean
to ascend through the creatures, or to seek the Beloved
　　　in them (as some would have it, for whom to seek
by night is to seek through creatures or through the traces
　　　of creatures)." By "visible creatures" he meant,
he explained, "the vestiges of God." I am almost
certain I have forgotten how to properly harness a horse.
　　　Skills leave the body of faith just as they leave the body
of culture, at a regular rate, which is why I spend
　　　my spare time reading obscure architectural histories.
　　　　Because math makes the mind smaller, perhaps.
Because the eye is always a lame master. "Try to fix
　　　the fiery planet in space. It is easy to make your own
tools," counseled the Romanian poet Gellu Naum.
　　　To place the self next to the self is the problem.
　　　　　The natives regard us soberly, relayed even further

from the blind pole: snip of hair, a mirror-grammar
        in pure water (bathing the saline body). Mandolin of ash
behind the green curtain. I recognize the wine
        when it is passed. I have only two hands. What, then,
                would you take from the dead? This is the perishable
text, not the ledgers filled with apocryphal jottings,
        flesh for knife, redress and return, face-down and known
by costume only (a name, an address, some reminiscence—
        broken off—a bawdy poem). I spotted the bones
                and admired as I always do their convex splay.
In the desert airport, opening and closing my eyes,
        as if something or someone would become even more
visible. But you pocketed the feather. And we kept
        walking, towards the ruins. We pass through and through,
                communicating jars with our bell-like tones.
It's night now. The bones glimmering like phosphorescent
        spiders, so still they seem to cast their own music.
The black fruit of the world (and its terrible blood).
        And yet the eye opening, cleanly into the clearing
                of matter. We strain our ears listening, as among thorns.
Such lucky beasts. Never to emerge on the other side.

CROYLAND ABBEY

irrigation or exit
November
the pearl presence
ensconced
in prayer's mouth
whose tongue, whose
seasonal apse
weeping
comes to ground
here, to rest
autumn's glands
milk their bronze
museum
comes the hour
of fasting, but
(in prayer's mouth)
the same water
only
without gravity's
percussive tyranny
breathe in
the marshes'
dank parliament
Ophelia
in the mystery cycle
is the first
to testify, blue riff

surfacing
the sky's drain
a better warden
perhaps
the concentric flocks
make their small
gauze
it's early
I have pierced
my inconsequence

MUTTER MUSEUM WITH OWL

*

The museum is meant to overwhelm: the profusion,
the arrangement, precept upon precept, line
upon line. The sheer weight of all those ingested
objects, deformed tibiae, trepanned skulls.
It's not the gore of it that upsets me, my friend
said, *but the rage to classify, to collect.*

*

Back on the street, or rather twelve or fourteen feet
above the foot traffic, the owl cocks its head,
looks steadily at one of us. Which? We can't all
belong here, language won't allow it, neither physics.
Speech's pathogen public in its wet mount—

*

The virus eats away at the bronze globe's
claustral flank. What's beautiful about corruption
are the maps it induces: clandestine autobiographies
re-inscribed in paler serum, the phantom wings
lifting against the moon's apse. Inside the bronze
a sister darkness grows, just a little closer.

*

The unseen parts of the eye crowd the edge
of the retinal plate—nobody asks what their pulse-
alphabets are busy unwriting. *Dance,*
hisses the body. *Dance,* echoes the absence
inside the globe. You catch this voice in a drop
of blood, suspended within winter's blue throat.

*

Things I've never asked my mother: did you ever
have a miscarriage, cheat on your husband,
see your father naked, dream in another language,
intentionally harm an animal. Is there
an animal you've never seen in waking life, that
you wanted to see. Do you have the falling
dream, do you like it when you have the falling
dream. When were you most hungry.

*

Screech, barn, great horned, saw-whet, barred—
Don't speak, said my friend. A novel clutches
more precisely at what speech is trying to say.
The grapes on the table glitter in the humidifying
pleroma: feast of argon, feast of tin. Tear
the veil away, earth's nude calendar of saints.

*

At last the voice is a fire; it hollows the face
into competing planes, acute angles
down which the living slide. The owl, the branch
from which it hung, one girder grasping another
in the city's doubled twilight, bleached
down to the master tones. Friend or phantom, prey
or predator, appetite has its own small god.

NATIVE, LIKE A QUINCE

Now I address the star
torn from the night's last wound.
Be a maul
unto me, I plead.
Pearl me & blacken me.

From the nerve
a bit of language creeps,
keratonous
like the eye's dark tooth & vine.

A little music
unspools the state's mirror.
The body, fungible, makes change.

I place a new stone
within the cairn's orbit,
cosecant.
I mix the fruit & the bread.

& the star says, *Swallow me.*

We lived together
as a lamp, in the city of lamps,
for many years.
A garment to the valve.

You are not to blame
for matter, I whisper, irradiant
as a prince.
—For what then.

For the road that leads
out of the city,
into the harvest of roots

the eye tenders.
That much, yes. That
& for what troubles
the face in the shuddering water.

NORTH WALSHAM

In a hotel in a small town in Norfolk I am listening to someone
throwing glass bottles into a metal bin: toss-shatter, toss-shatter.
There are no other sounds; it's a quiet afternoon
but the one tossing them has a sense of rhythm and I have
a sense that this has been going on for some very long time,
time being that medium through which we convey
the least knowledge of our circumstances to God, or one another,
which the body registers dimly in its cathedral of cells,
its telomeres, its intrinsically photosensitive retinal ganglia
that register the long days and longer nights of the blind.
There is pilgrimage and then there is direct action of the hand,
what Simone Weil called the "iron" at whose touch
"there must be a feeling of separation from God such as Christ
experienced, otherwise it is another God," toss-shatter,
the grasping and then relinquishing of the evidence of desire.
I was perfectly happy there said the famous writer of this place,
supposedly, when in fact it was a physician's surgery
(the physician was her friend; she came here to escape the city),
one young woman after another learning the art of venipuncture
and practicing it, for the public good. There was a time
when I had to keep track of which arm had most recently
offered blood. Outside a storm either is or is not billowing in
from the North Sea, from drowned Doggerland
into and over which I stared for several hours yesterday,
the Prussian blue-gray stain of the sky leaving the dark water
somehow lighter, as if possessed not of phosphorescence
but of resistance, a thunder-fetter. All afternoon I'd been followed
from ancient church to ancient church by two policemen
in a gaudy van; finally on some cliffs above the sea
I spoke to them, we exchanged cordial greetings and they sent me
on towards the bus stop at the outer edge of Mundesley

which, like Dunwich, is slowly slipping into that same depth.
I waited there with a woman and her child and a man who either
was her lover, or had been her lover, or—not the father
of her child—wanted to be her lover. "Tool and a closed vessel"
wrote Simone Weil. I admire her notebooks so much more
because they force the reading mind to draw inferences,
to make the leaps she couldn't quite force herself to make
except in the fictions of her final essays, and in her particular
end, itself a kind of fiction, a falsified denouement,
all clues leading to both act and actor, in perfect symmetry.
For now we can pretend she was a character in a book,
her own book, perhaps—her own cave (elsewise Plato's).
She who abhorred choice, who wrote "That is the whole problem.
To make time a moving image of eternity, for it is not so
naturally," toss-shatter, toss-shatter. What was once the tallest
church tower in Norfolk collapsed here in stages,
1724, 1835, 1836, and was not rebuilt. I think about the fact
that Siegfried Sassoon and I both contemplated this
meaningless antiquarian datum, but also the exquisite tiny fane
at Edingthorpe, that reels in the light cast by the sea
and unfamines it, somehow, forces the intelligence back inside
its nude bottle. "Make it so that time is a circle and not a line"
(Weil again) and "Here are certain things which cause no
suffering whatever by themselves, but make us suffer as signs."
She meant things like her Renault ID card, a soldier
in German uniform, a scrap of penmanship. *A hymn
veins the forest* is what I thought, at the time, and (—*I will have it
break my mouth).* What, then, of pilgrimage, that takes
the suffering sign and inscribes it over the length of the body
as a route, or, if you prefer, inscribes it *as* the body
over some distance in space, as a system of pain and arrival?
I admit I withdrew into my own small confession.

If like Weil we see God not *in* the injury, but *as* the injury
itself, the five Christs of Christ, each declaring its own gospel
according to its bloody lips, its bloody tongue—
A distant rectitude, where my book lay like some other
body I'd been wearing, or trying on, or trying to wear and then,
exhausted, set aside, too difficult, too meticulous for now.

BROKEN THINGS
Morwenstow

You stow them to the rear of worship: bits of jagged iron,
candle-nubs, miscellaneous gears and levers, each perfect
unto itself but useless apart from its fellows. The human
back is meant to bear this weight: cable spools, dusty
vases. Here is a picture of Christ, and here is a picture of
Christ. Imagine the eyes first, oblique timepieces upon
which vision prints. I cough up a tooth, mature and perfect.
It glistens in my hand. The chancel remains locked,
nursing its treasures with a dim milk. I can just feel the
tooth resting in the center of my palm; I shift it slightly,
its planes mazing the half-light. Is it broken, I ask myself.
Is it worship. Every century or four someone scrubs the
images from the walls and replaces them with new images.
A fish. A crown. A scythe. See, this special niche for
books from which pages have been torn. You may open
and close them: an almanac, a lab manual, a toddler's
pop-up fable. In my hand I am still holding this single
tooth, which my body offered up. It is not, to my knowledge,
mine. I imagine the dark chancel full of teeth, a mouth
sewn shut. GO FIND OUT THE ARROWS instructs
the legend in the glass, that falls on me. Nowhere is there
speech or talk of mending. A child's collage, a cracked
slate. I can't decide where to leave the tooth: in the Lady
Chapel, by the font, at the ad hoc altar to war veterans
in the north aisle. The tooth requires neither assembly nor
instruction. It is a cool kernel in my outstretched hand.
So I swallow the tooth. In this way I turn my back on
worship. I take it with me, away from the splintered table-
leg, the xylophone missing a key, the saints' tongues,
the floral wire, old kneelers with their stuffing leaking out.
Easter baskets, water pitchers. The damaged umbrellas.

NEVER-ENDING BELLS
Hartland, Devon

Peeping Tom through the gateway arch, above the combe,
    from the cliff that hides the sea's advent. We are made
        of stones today. It is a difficult office but no more
difficult than some. The stones grind against one another.
    You can hear this sound. It rides above the sea like a blind

halo. Peeping Tom is all eyes, a tower of eyes, in four
    stages. Which means: Peeping Tom is deaf. The sea
        bears every body eastward, until something stops it.
On the edge of the cliff I stop nothing. Sound waves
    move through me, bands of light penetrate the outer strata

of my tissues, both living and dead. At first I thought
    I was hearing things, a myth maybe. (Merely relieved
        they were not voices.) There is always the risk
of the body's betrayal, in a high place. I checked my wrists,
    my feet. I had no rope with me. I turned my back

to the sea, and there was Peeping Tom. I had almost forgotten.
    Thus this was the day of bread and fire. A small boat
        passed very close beneath me, its engine stuttering on
and off. I had the idea that there might be, after all, other
    worlds. But the distribution of waves in space is a science.

And the satellite dishes arrayed over the headland,
    answerable to every flux of intention. They are shapely,
        I admit. One can pass quite close to them. Even so,
it took me longer than it should have to meet the eye
    of the master. Because the eye is a fire to the hearing,

lays a fire on the ear's plank roof. Pierce the skin of the drum
and the flesh will do your hearing for you. Or so
I am told. The tower risen like a planet, unblinking,
above the horizon's inverse swell. The satellite station sieving
information, information. But shapely, *enormous*

crucified ghosts is what I thought. A flock disrobing
in the presence of matter, at the edge of great waters.
Peeping Tom concealing its peal of five until
the eye, like any other membrane, is spoken-*through,* becomes
not the perceiver but the medium through which

perception captivates. And I wanted to run there, I
wanted that communion, something every cell in my body
assented to. I stood motionless, fixed between sky
and sea and the starred wire with its tufts of dirty wool,
between the tower and the satellite dishes. The sea presses

its affirmation on everything it touches, *yes yes yes.* I felt
no hunger, in the natural man. The dream of time
stopping inside itself, stone within a stone within a stone.
I had read about the alloy but I had not really understood:
that like any animal I could be caught in a beam of light,

a sound, a flesh. A pinch of salt. Later I would want
to climb up into the eye, the voyeur's crystal socket. And
of course the door would be locked, the tumbler frozen.
And I would remain a man, turning again in realization
it was not some other world I'd thrilled to. It was this one.

SHALL BEAR UPON HIS SHOULDER IN THE TWILIGHT
—Eze. 12:12

Reaching from history, that alpenglow, towards the dead whose clothes I wear
tracked from room to room, the prodigy house we've built
from the ambient low-fi hum—You pass your tongue through it. But what *are* you,
the woman in the checkout line kept asking (watched over by the tabloids,
themselves an extinction event, a deferred ecology). What makes you permeable
to axe. Shelter. Effigy. Tarot. I place my hand inside the box
& then I draw it out again. (The film students worship in ragged pairs.)
In the carrion-fields the insect eye unpicks the red thread, its tiny miracle-play:
Split the body to expose the toll. So you step out into the diversity retreat
the faith calls "Easter." Someone else's memory, the jeweled slime of the carp's
underbelly, its torsion & snap. We loot the house of its unmentionables.
Today I wear the hat of a man whose daughter I did not marry
& the dark brown shirt of another man whose daughter did not marry me.
Music sifts through the otherwise empty room reserved for what we call the future,
though it isn't that. Almost imperceptibly my organs break
from the picture plane, the finance sector, the matte radio whose sticky
wave-fronts buy the body back. —That's what it wants. What it always wanted.

ON THE FEAST OF THE HOLY INFANTS KILLED FOR CHRIST'S SAKE IN BETHLEHEM

It is banal to return to the past but a past is all I have. Things in their presence speak
to other things: the coffee pot, the crust of earth by the cemetery drop.
If there's a gap then there must be a witness. So like flame to make its home
among us, to insist it does not destroy. I try to take it in my hand
with the usual result. Part of me is now estranged from the absurd collective
comity of cells, of bodily recompense. The past imputes a language; indeed,
only the past may impute a language, any legibility of the tongue.
Some people marched here. Some of them held up a body. Exalt the body
in a public place, is what the blood wants. And we were so kind to it,
we petted it and fed it and then doffed our wool caps at the elements, each in turn.
It is banal to refer to them as "the elements," air and fire, earth and water.
In the past we had better names, which do not now exist except
applied to quantity, to volume, fine transpiercings. I drew a steel splinter
into my hand and then, a week later, I drew it out again. It fell almost immediately
away from me, from where I could see it, and I felt inexplicably
grieved. Steel is the best of what fire leaves in our care. One can build with steel,
one can build with stone. Steel speaks to stone, while I huddle inside
my carbon plank. I hear nothing but the past, its obtuse echolalia.
Skill is to know where the gun, fired, will strike the body, where and what
the knife, deployed, will cut. Clerks record what happens next, all now in the past.
I watch the winter snow withdraw into what we call the new year,
listen at my paneled wall for the tranced hive. My lost organs return to me
in dreams; they speak in unknown tongues. I judge them holy. I judge them saints.
Then I bend to the Psalms again. I try each in the sharp light,
drop it back into its rosewood box. *Did you see,* it mutters to its fellows.
Did you see that, did you hear. The gossip of the Psalms is banal:
ancient feuds, agonies, indiscretions, existential trauma
induced as false labor, a few torn and dirty epithets. I lift the rake from its stirrup
and begin churning the wet leaves. There is more body here than I or anyone
quite knows what to do with. And yet we are careful, so very careful.
What I love about the past is that it does not break. It is breakage. It is broken.

IN HIM WERE HIDDEN ALL OUR TONGUES
Cliffside, N.C., 2015

Abide with me. Zion is wasted and these mowers
move each like an abandoned church across this grass-scape,
replete in their genitals. Magnolia-sire, your faith
is in my mouth below the ruined Baptist church. I am buying,
I am selling, I cannot think for all the roses that have died
for me, for me, taking this block wall. This rail. This cracked
asphalt. A little higher, a little lower, my friend Theologian,
borne up on your memorized flood. Inside the frame

chapel, a single shadow (white) and another shadow (black)
and all along a single bell, canted and ringing. This is not
about responsibility. This is not about the post office,
the Masonic Lodge so extant they repel the sun. There is always
a point of entry into the church of the body, which is
sometimes furnished, sometimes not. Imagine the arms
of the men and women carrying the last flowers
from this building masquerading as my funeral. My dramatis

personae. You see, when a body carries something before it
the hands, the tips of the hands move into the future first.
And there is a certain looseness, a certain bend
to the knee. So you can still send a letter there, suitably
franked. Trespass is possible. Replace the houses with trailers
and feel if not *good* about it, then at least *strong.*
Able to wield any tool, to mow in season. Male and female
the mowers, scattered now across the apron of the hill. Soon

I will almost remember where I am, the great bruise
called Art dredged up from the deep tissues of history,
that ravished mirror. My parents said *they worked for hours
and hours, as if they were guests.* "Worked like guests"

is what I heard. I could have watched their children playing
in the sandpit by the school, but that would have been
wrong. Behind the next hill crouches a low building
now labeled THE CHURCH OF THE EXCEPTIONAL

("For the Physically & Mentally Handicapped")
which I am quite sure used to be something else. Pentecostal?
Wheels within wheels sing the mowers, chanty-style,
but there's no one to answer, the children having been
led blindfolded back into the school. I'm not making this up
and I'm not grieving. I have just broken off a blade of palmetto
and rolled it between my fingers, which are the future
we share, the difference between what is priestly

and what is merely priest. Flowering and unflowering
in the heat of the day, its fat, percussive knot.
Paint an angry moon on the door if you think it would help.
There is not enough marriage imagery in the world
of this poem, my lame accountant told me, after the fact.
I'd ask the mowers, but they have fled from me now,
into the shade of their noonday meal. Set the first gate
beneath the night's jute skin. I have drawn you a map of what

is most fallow within me, where the altars once stood.
The time I vaulted the railing to save the boy whose polyester
robe had leapt up in flame—and the time I did not.
The time I merely watched, to see what would happen next.
These grasses are what happens next, and the high places
from which our lives run down like definitions, *parable*
and *blastocyst* and *felon*. There are no hunters here because it is not
the season for hunting. My knowledge takes me this far,

as far as the calluses between forefinger and thumb.
Desolate and void the master sang, but so beautifully I wanted
to follow him. I followed him. And through me passed men
and women, their arms all held out, not in supplication
or welcome but in the bearing of burdens. Abide with me,
O you pretty adoption. I will be your map. I will lift your body.
I am gathering the grass of you into my arms right now.
Don't listen to the mowers, or to the songs their children sing.

BLUE HERON, MARLBOROUGH

Just yesterday I thought, it's as if almost three years of my life
vanished, in a mist, the memories are both partial and distorted,
who was that person, what was I thinking, what did I say,
days and months went by this way, years, I wrote a few poems,
even more the poems that went unwritten, and then I drove
to the singing this morning, in the hall by the deep river
about which I've dreamed intermittently since 2004, at least
when I was dreaming, before that too was taken from me,

outside it was overcast and then it was raining again but music
was still present to succor us, I could throw myself
into music, into the act of others throwing themselves, this
was a tiny nation I had pledged fealty to long ago, it was like
reciting the Pledge of Allegiance except with bells in the throat,
I thought, *of all days,* I thought, some of the people
in this large room I will never meet, will never know, others
I've known for more than half my life, I was drowsy and then

my voice failed and I moved from the front row to the back,
remembering Carl Carmer and his journey through Alabama
in an election year, that made everything a candidate,
the young woman in the orange dress on the front pew
of that clapboard church, not quite like this (this rented hall)
but the women here favor print dresses and it's close enough,
the tossing of the head, the hair, my vocal cords descended
into the hell of the body and came up singing, then they froze,

it was a single choking motion, I was making a sound
and then I wasn't, and the rain mizzled off, I was driving
back through the mist, an actual mist, it was as if
having stumbled up to some acme, some point of vantage,

I had plunged back down again into sightlessness, or perhaps
the mist had shifted, I had outraced it for a moment,
gotten ahead or behind it, the superposition, I could see
clearly the landscape of my life, the little farms and villages

with their monuments and hardware stores, I wasn't part
of the scene because I was at this high clear elevation,
I thought, *I can remember imagining my life,* I can just recall
what it felt like to work, to plan, to make of myself
a thread in the bright tapestry, before it was snatched back,
I could feel my life hopelessly disclosed, swept past,
I don't even remember the townships I drove through
(the map ticks their names: Sunderland, Montague, Erving,

Northfield, Winchester, Swanzey, Keene), and then
the eye's pattern recognition software kicked in, it was one
of the bogs I had no name for, they were just bogs
hemmed in between Marlborough and Dublin, flag-plaqued
before the nice houses of Dublin and the bona fide lakes,
there was nothing there, lush reed beds in the mist,
it was entirely unremarkable, but in the flicker of my passage
I remembered I had seen an enormous blue heron

once, on the north side of the road (New Hampshire 101),
precisely there, stalking something in the blackish
water, this could have been 2001 or 2006 or 2012,
there's no way to tell, the mind filed it under "miscellaneous,"
the mind filed it under "icon," under "rubbish," the mind
filed it under "evidence for the existence of God,
q.v.," I was flipping pages to find the proper reference
when the mist seized everything again, I remember wanting

something so badly, and then—not wanting, and then merely
moving about in a landscape that had been scarred
by music, by the making and then the memory of music,
by the rare earth elements that had been necessary
to reproduce that music, to make it more widely available, music
you see was for a time one of the few things that penetrated
the mist, I left the hall before the singing was over,
it was late and I convinced myself I had to be somewhere

else, by 5, I missed the prayers and the announcements,
I was already back in the mist, could feel it thrumming
where my vocal cords had been, raw and terrible, other people
were setting up their barbecues in the countryside
and readying themselves for the fireworks, I thought vaguely
how it's always best to avoid the valley towns on the days
of the old pagan festivals, this is ancient prudence, and then
the mind remembered, the mind placed its polarized

glass on top of what the eye perceived, it was like that,
a black-body problem, I nearly veered from the pavement,
it was not quite dusk and the bones of the dead lay perfectly
in their respectable graves, those at least who were dead,
who were respectably dead, I kept passing their white stones,
their whitewashed demesnes, what I am telling you now
is that the first thing to pour back through that dank gate
was neither choice nor joy nor reason, but a terrible hunger—

JONES MOUNTAIN ECLOGUE

First hard freeze. Night for the setting of traps. So what if the dialogue
was about sexual possession, in the end? Apophony, plasmic trinity
of sound moving away from the body. And why must we use honey,
you asked. Because it is expensive and because it scathes the soul, I replied.
We could hear dead voices in the distance. That which is sweetness
corrects for that which is death. No I would never value the roses
more than Christ, I thought. (Because what if the dialogue is about sexual
possession, in the end?) Because it is my name day and I am very tired.
The honey she sent me, from across an ocean. Its brittle vial. Because
my mother called to remind me what the weather was like while
she lay in the hospital giving birth to me, to my body. A rhetorical form
that concedes sleep's shapeliness. I can't remember the name of that place
I want to *stay,* she kept repeating. While knives were distributed
to children. I test my breath on the lathe of the night air; it hums. So,
"the merciless recurrence of our nakedness" (Ann Lauterbach).
But we were brought here by such splendid vanities, I protested. The Christ
for which Nineveh waited. The errancy. Spread before the congregation
like swaths of ivory chenille. It is not that we are possessed, but that
some vagrance hunts us. And then what had been my soul leapt within me,
exultant. Each of the stars in the cemetery raises its five-fingered
fraction to me. We are all coffins for your scent, they sing. I'm burned
from listening to them; the tender flesh of my inner ears shines with scars.
I am afraid of sleep's charcoal sketch. If only I could give my blood
away, I murmured to the winter hives. Now dawn's blue night-wrist opens.
The native name for this mirror is breath, my physician insists. First
hard freeze, first glass tone. I go to him carrying my cities in my hands.

THE CONSTELLATIONS

Compress for me, portraits of the Fathers induced in oils
    against the Art Deco wainscoting, the mote in God's
        efference recedes, a remnant, a sail settled deep
    into the history of gold thread, Klimt swarming gargantuously
at the eaves, *adore & propagate,* we were dispersed
    in a wood, it was more dank than dark but I could not
        distinguish your face from the faces of others
(it was or seemed to me then a crowded wood, as in a war,

after a pitched battle singly & in small groups refugees creep
    into the forest), chiefly I knew you by your smell,
        its hint of vanilla, everything overhead was obscured
    by some greater paroxysm, I had become sky-deaf, anyway
it was dusk, I desperately wanted music, not to make music
    myself perhaps but for someone to make it for me,
        for there to *be* music, but the only sound
beneath that violent heaven was the susurration of branches,

of limbs as we brushed them, as we were brushed, it seems
    we went on for hours in this way, I patted my pockets
        over & over for the lump of candle you'd handed me
    in those last moments before our journey
began, sometimes it was there, sometimes it wasn't, a nub of wax
    with a blackened thread, how much better if it had been
        edible, a crust or cheese, or else an heirloom, my great-
grandfather's lead plumb-bob, its spatchcocked swan, from

behind someone moaned a little, perhaps it was you, maybe
    I'd gotten ahead of you, it was difficult to tell, bright flashes
        overhead suggested the Judgment in one form or another
    but that had nothing to do with me, with us,
I did not feel frightened, only urgent, it was so important
    that we keep moving, that the calendar include
        this day, fringed with rooks, & before, things like
carrot soup, the chipped case of a piano, the operetta score

by the young composer that someone at some point
    left out in a drizzle, oddly although there were no roads,
        no clear path we did not seem to have too much trouble
    making our respective ways forward, *towards the caves*
it occurred to me, without acknowledging that the last cave
    I had visited had been under a castle & the one before that
        hidden deep in childhood's erstwhile kleptomanias,
you're lying on a bed in a fever you can't quite recall,

you haven't been overtaken by manliness yet but you know
    about it, you've inferred it from your own father,
        he's not there & he won't be but you're not frightened,
    if you could lift your right arm you could touch
the fine red hairs of the animals gathered around you
    which in retrospect resemble lynxes but probably aren't
        because they circulate too silently, too fluidly,
they don't seem dangerous but then another dark branch

whips back against your face & you're in the forest again
 stepping into what appears to be a clearing, it's night now
  & when you glance up you notice, as if for the first time,
 the constellations, they're so beautiful, so abstract
& so narrative, the plough which could be a transport
 which could be a bear & keeps flickering on & off
  like a defective neon sign seen from an almost infinite
prescience, the twin rabbits holding their silver bows,

the Abbey Gate, these all circle too but still I'm not frightened,
 the butchery is far behind us & thus far we've made
  excellent time, all things considered, this would be
a good place to return in winter, to see the scripts a frost
might practice, or in spring for mushrooms, it has that sense
 of "a good place," I accept a shovel from someone
  & start digging in the illuminated darkness, it's tradition
that everyone take his turn, it feels good to add a little Kiev,

a little Prague to this flint-pocked ground, I recall perfectly
 the first time I felt your hair (in my hands I mean),
  what it felt like to run your hair through my heavy hands,
 I must remember to bait the traps is what I'm thinking
& about the minor third in the aria I may never hear again,
 in the operetta by the young composer, when I realize
  suddenly I'm just a bit chilled, the woods are quiet now
& I want to kiss you, or at least show you, but you're not there—

ON BEING MISTAKEN FOR "PART OF THE ART" AT THE MATTRESS FACTORY MUSEUM IN PITTSBURGH

The orderly shaved my chest to make way for the electrodes.
Later, I was mistaken for part of an artwork by an artist
I'd long admired—not once, not twice, but three times.
"I'm so sorry," one woman said. The third woman screamed,
which caused her boyfriend to scream. I admit I'd been sitting
very still—there's no rule against sitting very still inside
an artwork that includes a functional chair. I'd been thinking
about light, and the ways light affects my ideas about dwelling,
about belonging as a function of topography, of space.
Both planets and buses revolved around me, around where I sat
in the artist's contrived dusk. After the electrodes, I'd noticed
my shirts felt different, nestled against my half-shaved
torso—the first time I'd felt that particular texture, sensation,
in thirty years. It was something I noticed standing up
and sitting down. It was something I noticed at my desk,
and in the cemetery that lies between the house in which I live
and the school at which I teach. Years ago I'd researched
the lives of the women and men whose graves I pass
each day: the woolen factory owner, the canal boatman,
the expatriate bandleader from Mauritius. Lawyers, doctors,
the lone Confederate soldier whose invisible partisans
remember him with a flag every autumn. I've photographed
that flag; once I even stole it, from the grave, and discarded it
by night. This could have been an artwork, and I
could have been in it, legitimately. I sat in the faux dusk
and watched as projections played against dollhouse facades,
gantries and churches culled from model railway sets.
In the distance an ancient wheel clanked as it revolved.
Men and women had lived in that place, the last three names

still etched above brass mailboxes in the derelict foyer.
Don't worry, the orderly had told me, it will grow back—
it will just seem strange, for a little while. Images
of my viscera played on the screen above where we could all
see them, him, me, the two nurses in attendance. When I
was a boy I found my father's ratty stash of Jacquard
loom patterns in the attic, his Boy Scout merit badge cards
from before he had to drop out to work in the mill. The artist's
installation included a soundtrack, creepy one-handed
piano music punctuated by the barks of hammers, the whines
of saws. The last time I visited my father in the mill—
a different mill—my ears rang for hours from the weave
room racket. Don't worry, the night shift overseer told me,
it only causes damage in the higher registers, and it's not
like our employees listen to classical music or anything.
This was in Halifax, Virginia, one town north of the hospital
where I'd been born. We visited as a troop; I earned
that badge, even as I began to suspect that if I ate their food,
drank their mead, I would never leave that place. Earlier,
I'd sat in complete silence and darkness for twenty minutes,
waiting for my eyes to adjust. And there, just ahead,
the milky, almost-absent gauze that represents the Pleiades
rushing away from everything we know, deeper into
the night sky. I'd wanted, as a youth, to be an astrophysicist,
that I might know distance better. In the end the math
eluded me. I was then very far from home, as I now am
in a city where steel was once made, and where my mother's
half-brother lies in an unmarked grave. One can know
these things, theoretically; one can document. Dennis Maher's
installation was entitled *A Second Home.* The Turrell
piece was his *Pleiades,* from which I eventually fled
because I wearied of warning others in that all-but-darkness
"To your left, somebody here." One cursed me as I sat
in the plastic chair. I liked, in the Maher, the obsessive sense

that space fills space, the claustrophobia towards which
the third woman reached, as much to the belated realization
that I was breathing, I was a man, I could still move my arms
and legs. When people tell me they remember certain
physical sensations, I know they're lying. We only recall
having felt, whether pain or pleasure, the snug embrace
of a 40% polyester shirt against bare skin so plain
each time we forget about it until, having stumbled hard
in the whitewashed corridor, the body experiences it anew.

ONLY COERCE YOURSELF GENTLY, & SHOW

Bald Eagle State Forest, Pennsylvania

I write about "the eye" because you will not accept "faith"
or "the soul." Make it milk, then, the vitreous humor. The chicory
& the sassafras: you could declare a home here. Blazed red
among the laurels. "Almost invisible," read the guide (unhelpfully,
I'd thought: but accurate). Almost a faith, almost a soul,

almost a slow turning. The eye, blazoning amid the laurel.
Even the tumbling of the waters has fled from me. What is there
to say "no" to, here. *Penthos,* cried the old men of the desert
(I stagger my steps). A richness among the threads. Raveling &
unraveling. Later I find Shriner Mountain on my map; that is to say

I entered the wilderness alone. In the time of witnesses.
I was reading the letters of friends (in the desert), I was drunk
with moss. Lay your veil over me, bridesman. Your lush creed
from which the insects sip as they do also from my blood
("almost invisible"). Plastered underneath the body (of the beloved.

(Where the young men laid down their arms. Where motion
struck me)). The acorns pale green in this season of vertical alms,
cupped in greener hands. What is deciduous vs. what is
not—the long, pendentive barrows of the saints. And mark me.
Who have ascended through vestiges of the hunt. The durable blaze

& its beastly reckoning. Never say orator, but: in priestly intercept.
My small art draws upward (from decay (of this body (&
others))). Almost a perfect temple, the Amanita. Those that draw:
either to consume or to defend (lead kindly). Thus strode I
Host to the hostless in the day of my unfastening. Astray now, &

in plain view. Keep this ledger for the stillest warden. The venous
eye, carrying back all that has been depleted.
Yesterday in the cemetery the soldiers fired once, twice,
three times. I say "the eye," because the spirit of this age is round.
No longer can the past be claimed to other us. I must imagine

what it would be like to be hungry, here—I, dressed all in blue
but ignorant of every feast save my mammal-smell.
Who am perceived not in depth but in manner. Behind me
something breaks athwart the deadfall. It is a tremendous thing,
the weight of oxygen against a davening blood. The laurel

presses me with its oil; the young sassafras anoints. My eye
(read heart), my soul (read eye)—with the hardwoods in their spec-
tral shift, their flush concordance. Let them gaze into that
which I can never be. I am not the only worker in the forest, merely
the blindest. See what letters I brush with my crude hands.

(WORDWELL I)

chronic lapse
birdsong

& because
everything
does separate,
the grasses

(their mute
understudies)

chronic lapse
that touches
the soft break

three, four

three, four

beat
the pattern
the ripe air

scrollwork
to the eye's
studded
tympanum

that breathes

welcome
oh, welcome

where
are you going
where
have you been

(WORDWELL II)

place your fingertip
into the shallow
depression, the drain

(I rise, I do this: see)

make bread of me
the air pleads, kneading
its wide-open wound

(I rise, I
place my finger in it)

is your name
Light, then (says the air)
No, I reply (&
take my seat again)

is your name
Breath (closer. I sign
my grief
into the Book of Griefs)

let's wipe out
the birds
together, the air suggests

let's place
our fingers into
the shallow depression
each bird's body
makes

No, I tell the air
Wait here

—*Yes,* the air agrees

(I rise, I drink
the flags
to their bitter dregs)

(WORDWELL III)

I will wake some
blood
for you, the air
said (helpfully,
it seemed to think,
from its tone)

No thank you,
I responded

I have woken
enough blood
already, by myself

Then let me
put it to sleep,
the air offered,
I know
such fine lullabies

No, thank you
I said again,
testing
the iron hinges

(this was my
blood's dream,
I woke
with my blood's
dream in my

mouth, on all
my flushed faces)

ON HEARING A CUCKOO AT PENTECOST
Lackford

You are not brave. But what does bravery mean, here. Tongues of fire
distributed like so many paper crowns. Little flames, permitting heat, light.
That is what you are, hidden in your narrow band of wood.
You have stolen something
again. You may be held responsible.
Your one note of bargaining, your other note of faith, a garland
that seizes what it paraphrases.
You are not aware of any ruin. Or, you *are* ruin,
perched inside the ripe conflagration, its emerald knot. A thinking jewel.
What must it be like, to know oneself for what one really is.
Bravery has no part in it. The flame
extending as far down as the tongue, the human member, but no further.

PENTECOST, RISBY

Ask the cut lilacs what "safety," what "suffering" mean.
They strike the drain with their feeble crosses. It is like watching
honey writhe, a spasming flag. Everything otherwise is very still.
Faith has left this place & taken its ragged choir with it,
its urchins & its bells. I want to touch the butchered blossoms,
so I do. This is not a metaphor. They are in this place
just as the shadows of dogs are in this place. Tally the soldiers
lost for this, who limp along the bridleways. Their cries
are bits of glass. They are known by the sun as well, but this
is the moon's fable, carved from every tangent limb. Moist
do we enter & moist are we borne away. I touch the lilac
once more, its fading neume. I wish music were the friend (to us)
it pretends to be. Such vagrant architectures. Captain, we are
very small, our ships have been examined by eminent physicians
who find no fault. Let the tongue rest now, for awhile.
Let it shear its long dream from the bodies of sheep, or wolves.
We never know whose corpse we are wearing, whose dead.

[WEST STOW ORCHARD (I)]

I limped into the orchard. I was not in what I thought of as pain. I admit
I was comforted by the walls, which brought to mind the virtues.

The kind eye, that suffers movement. The kind wind, & the wind's blind
tongue.

I will never be so removed from consequence as I am now, is what I
thought.

I held silence as in my palm, watched it stretch, flex. I dressed my vocation
in rags, as one would a doll. (If one were a child.)

The children are engaged in naming. They chant *apple, apple, cherry,
pear, pear* as if they knew these things, green knots on arrayed
stanchions.

I make the circuit once, twice. I break the light.

Kind wind, the children have a message for you.

The witnesses pass through the galleries of oxygen, lithe forms. I do not, I
will not name names. (No, not even you, carpenter.)

A glass mask left in the care of strangers, I thought I heard the visiting
Canadian say. —But it sang, his wife protested. I heard it sing, I
heard its song.

(Kind wind braiding the orchard's laden limbs. Distant lorries on the
Brandon road.)

I am at the edge of all things, here. Or, all things have moved away from
me, at their proper & respective distances.

Distance of *was.* Distance of legible syntax.

There will be no touching, for a little while (I tell the roadkill owl).

My host says 10% of all carrots consumed on this island are grown on the
neighboring estate.

Think of the forest as memory, I tell the visiting Canadian (& his wife). An
ambient place some birds recognize. They have heard all the stories:

The one, for instance, about the crow & the golden comb. That starts &

stops, & then starts again, as if from some beginning.

I lean forward, into the pear tree's umbra. Like an equation, washable, wearable, something to cover the body.

Blood is the most local real estate, yes. The film the blood is showing to the children & wolves among the winter trunks, the winter hives.

And I drew philosophy up again from its hell of categories, I examined it. The pear tree's shadow clinging to me, to the hairs of my beard.

And I was not in pain, not in any way I could have described.

Revival is a kind of light, then, isn't it, the Canadian's wife pressed. We were silent for a time, though the dusk wasn't, its looping, avian life.

They, who know what marriage is; they, who tend the hidden ring, & that ring's thefts in the city of form. (Which is an empty, ruined city, though the tourist guides extol it.)

A single star leapt the wire fence, then subsided, back into the mirror.

We brought the mirror with us, my hosts said, simply. And the beautiful door, imported from the continent, such fine carvings.

I added more pigment to the palette, swirled it around. For the earth's banner, its iris-flag, a deep indigo; malachite for pride. Chalk for the unripe fruits.

And so I drew from that place a reticence, as from the deck of reticence. It lodged in my body, guest within guest.

Do you trust it, my hosts asked me, then. —I ask only that nothing happen twice.

[WEST STOW ORCHARD (II)]

I'd never thought of myself as cruel, before. (What's in the box? I heard her
  ask. Snake, fruit, text.)

How perfectly round permission is, like a plate, or a cork.

Set the meal, then. Gild the legible channels.

I paused on the bridge; I slowed my breathing, held my breath. Any name.
  Every name.

Even in winter, I doubted.

She said, When you say *pear,* I see *p-e-a-r* for a second before I see, in my
  mind's eye, a pear.

I measured the echo of your voice in inches, yards. It was a yellow roof.

She said, The clips of the soldiers in the trenches, surely you know them,
  everyone does—

So you see they hired a forensic lip-reader. To know, finally, what they were
  saying. (A century late, I offered.)

I glimpsed a great hand running itself, as it were, over the landscape. As if
  in warning, or in pleasure. Or both.

But the dreams receded yet again; I woke to everyday perfection.

Empty dream, empty space-of-dream the drugs whisk clear.

Let us set the wave offering, the heave offering at the blind center of the
  white room. —There. The birds circle less fitfully, their dull eyes
  track the throat.

I turn all the other beasts away.

There is no reason to read this, no reason to betray winter's final treaty.

The dream of the bridge, vs. the actual bridge; the song, vs. the actual song.
  The dream of breath, vs. actual breath: *takes hold.*

And here now are the dolls. Can you tell me what they are wearing? (Don't
  tell me what they are saying, what you dream they're saying.)

We stood in the rebuilt cloister & competed to see who had the most
  residual Latin.

By then, war's cowl had fallen away, revealing its pure animal mask. Blink
  once for *twice,* blink *yes* for *dog.*

Pace the blossom's cloister, its barred estate. Lupine, cyclamen, columbine
   calling for one another, across the walled garden.
There should be bells, she said. —Bells, then.
I couldn't find the clasped arms in the churchyard masonry, their blank-faced
   knot, the seven arguments for scale.
One thing becomes another. That city disappears into scissel, orchard, flood,
   six thousand dispossessions.
To lie face-down, by choice, on ground where other men have stumbled,
   fallen.
What's in the box, you ask: lace, owl, sun. The smoke of an hour. All I wanted,
   both then & later.
Spell it again, you tell me, only this time more slowly.

DENIZEN (WEST STOW ORCHARD)

On the postcard I etched a brief grief; I signed my name. She was not her doubts; she was not her manifested words. I stroked the cheek of one who had transcribed the radioactivity of silk, who had drawn a coin from the fodder (that fable). As per chronicle, no hell abandoned its ark to full height. But we are *handled*—the saints brush each of us, little lessons in gravity they apparently need. Blue herons, the pair I startled, could be dead by now, I can't know. The heath mist treating as if in friendship. My friend's wife's absconded mind. The cost of that unfurnished house, versus the surgery. Dig until the bedrock stops you. Let's give gifts of honey this winter, let's remember friends as we might the dead, let's let them in. Apply coals to their pale cloaks, their paler skins. Offer them a javelin from the collection. As for God, trapped inside the crevice I thought He passed by: once, twice, I hid myself, & my language. Of insufficient number who should thrive. The wound & its fury sheathed us. The angels compromise, their tight joins suborning the prosecutor's bride. Friend, tell me about your country, whether blood is acknowledged as currency, whether the children eat meat. It's true, I've handled snakes, but never in the context of faith. The slow death of the insects disturbed me, I admit. Cruelty had not been my intention. I pass the nails back down the row, as instructed. It's midnight again. Even the children have been taught to know how & whom to blame.

[WEST STOW ORCHARD (III)]

My Orthodox friend told me "Yes, we know, you want to be annihilated. All your work points toward this."

We were standing in her kitchen. It was late autumn, my natal season. I held a key in my hand.

That is the problem with listening, why stones refuse to do it, categorically.

I, being no stone, checked first my left lung, then my right. My liver, my kidneys, my spleen.

I had, by this time, relinquished several organs, but not these. These stood with me, drifts of foliage in the coppice of the body.

I dream, sometimes, of my missing organs, & of their harvesters. We miss each other.

The moat ran here, my host's husband explained, gesturing with his long arm. I dreamed I'd sleepwalked, though I hadn't.

Where the blood pools, the lymph: blocked channels. The body amending itself.

I admired the beautiful pottery on the ancient shelves, & then the shelves themselves for their own sturdy, wooden sakes.

Later, I sat as close to the apple bough as I could, without touching it. A breeze did the rest.

Time is a form of attention, no more, no less. Bodies record not time's many passages, but a brief of their attentions, a chronicle.

I focused as fiercely as I could on a single glass of water, as I would have on a god. But the key, warm now, set its imprint in my palm.

"Are you listening," my friend had asked.

The geometrical tracery in certain churches echoed by much later graffiti, its scrim of presence. Perhaps a belief in the magic of the body, perhaps not.

To register presence is also, at least hypothetically, to permit
absence, the possibility of absence, ghost dances under the
wide, moon-lit Septuagint.

I stepped once again beneath the orchard's chronic tent. *Permit,
sir, these narrow dead to speak, sir. A moment, sir—*

I envy every life that takes its root along a wall: lichen, toadflax. I
brush the apple blossoms from my sleeve, my vest.

Every figure in the landscape comes alive as trace, as function.
The orchard veers & parries.

Not an image but a true thing, *in language*. This was John's
argument, that he carried towards his Christ.

The truth is, I never wished for any higher office than presence.

But it was you who brought us here, your key I left that day on
the polished granite counter laden with olives, bread, sliced
kiwi, pomegranate.

Now I apprentice myself to disappearance, which is not the same
as annihilation. I still recognize Latin verb tenses when I
read them.

The apple boughs undulate in the Suffolk breeze, to which they're
bred.

Their attentions focused, coiled, splayed springs in the light. Into
which I, also present, also rise.

[WEST STOW ORCHARD (IV)]

I reckoned departure's latch, a green turning. The list of poets who were never in this place is a long one: Hopkins, Sappho, Stein. What has broken in you, a voice asked. In this season of late blossom. The yew appears, flickers, disappears again. Light's tricky syntax. I will not ascribe words to other beings (I wrote, in the sky's chalk, 100 times). But aren't you lonely, my hosts asked. Don't you need anything. Departure's latch, which requests the pleasure of your hand. No one has died more than twice. But the hand of the artist leaves us, again & again, with every work of art, every labor. It flies, as if into a mist. And there is beauty in this, as they say—& terror. I scratch at the insect bite on my right wrist. Every desire is blameless. The amputated stoup in the churchyard latterly a mounting block for the vicar, the guidebook informs. Or, the exquisite bindings of certain books. The wind is nobody's camera. Click & whir of its non-shutter. Nothing is more real than I presume it to be, here, now. (And you with me, perhaps just arriving, reach out to stroke the wisteria.) (Reach out & share the fluent shearling, the flow & glut of it.) I held the compass up to the mirror, then shook it, hard. In my dream I tried to explain my fever, my chills, my night sweats to the other communicants. No burials are scheduled for today, I heard the warden tell the sexton. Abolish the halocline, wake the sea up. That part of the sea that resides in the eye: that much, at least. I flicked an aphid from my blue sleeve. (And you are here, & you.) Little pageant of history's dire poverty, up against the blind gate. Irradiant vivisection of the body, & of its emblems. Hildegard's gnostic syllabary, through which she refreshed the true names, or so she claimed. Green latch in prime Suffolk light. It seems almost to breathe (as most things do). A rook gnaws it & then, startled, soars off. I recalled my days in the old capital. I dreamt I helped my hosts hang out my laundry, to dry.

[WEST STOW ORCHARD (V)]

So much for the portrait of continuous life, of what is shareable
or shared. My little debts, which I peddle in the marketplace:
carmine, turquoise, viridian. Recall the tabulation of the saints,
& their stippled reliquaries; let them bask in the late morning
glow, like music. (Like music only the blind can hear, I almost
wrote.) My little ships—sight, hearing, the organs' lordly drone—
goodbye, goodbye. I have provisioned you with nothingness. I
have not excluded the distant rumble of the expatriate airfield.
If we were visited by angels, how would we know (my friend
asked, earnestly). Continuous life: not the series of tones, but their
advents & dissolutions, imbricating. They're sewn from my tissues,
yes. Meanwhile the biographies accumulate, flotsam against
the drain's iron catch. Even more the unwritten biographies, of
course. Transposition of key: one of the distinct alchemies, his
account of the failed expedition, hers of that summer in France.
I signed no pacts as a child: of this much, at least, I am certain.
Only my misplaced faith in the mechanism, like a dancer's or an
athlete's. My little misplaced faiths, alive, alive-O. Where I will be
buried remains a question. But not for me, as I understand it. Sails
shapely as their crafts move away from us. By the ancient track a
child's mitten, a mylar party balloon, magenta, deflated. Should I
then drink more from consensus's cup, its undertone. The shore
makes the loneliest sound, independent of the succoring sea.

TO THE BANK HOLIDAY CARAVANS
IN EASTNOR PARK

You look like tinfoil, not the shook kind that both conceals and
    makes manifest
God's glory, but that other kind, the inside wrappers of candy bars
    eaten weeks, months
ago, twisted bits encrusted with leftover pie juices. Even the birds
    know to avoid
you. You are all queued in staggered ranks along the green hillside,
    as if waiting
to view an eclipse. But the declining sun is whole, today; the
    curtain
stays down, the movie will not start. I watch your wives, your
    children, your dogs
(for there are always dogs) even as I keep my distance. When you
    look up at the sun,
come now lately at evening after heavy rain, you look straight
    through me.
I never longed for this gift, nor, covered in mud and bruises, the
    steps that led me
back to this place while you, suffused with barbecues in drizzle,
    waited.
For you know about waiting, better than I. I have watched you
    wait, I who own
no patience—I have leaned against the cool glass and watched.
    When I turned away
it was to seek some new thing. But you remain (for a little while)
    where I left you,
a fleet of kings waiting quietly to present their gifts, as to some
    absent god.

[ST MELANGELL'S DAY, EASTNOR (I)]

The body and its members sway in time with the blood's beat,
its willing course. I brought the doves to the marketplace
in a wicker basket, to honor the museum's anniversary.
The shock of recognition effaces the particular, oaks, stones,
each bearing its private inscription. Say a poem is like that,
a bit of silence the world acceded to, for a finite duration.
Say a little bit of everything one takes into one's hands
remains, the pot smeared with soot, the Mazzolino canvas,
the ripe pear with its pesticide sheen. No other way to play it:
I had begun again, disremarked by the other guests
who stood around the floral displays, talking so animatedly.
Outside it was raining. In my pocket the stub of a ticket,
a pause my fingers idly groped. In the corbels, identical beasts
devoured one another. And I thought, yes, it is like that,
as much as any thing can be like another thing; I thought,
the canon of matter is so vast, it keeps imprinting
its judgments on both guests and hosts. For I was a guest,
as I kept reminding myself, striding away from that dim town.
I copied myself into the legend, not with the strength
of iron gall but such that others, who would come after me,
might scrape the surface and apply their own insignias,
their own ludic anthems fleeing to the skirts of some Welsh
saint, as if she might protect them. As if she understood
their language. And in the negotiations that followed,
the tense exchanges (hollow apart from their brackish rinds),
a tongue precipitates. It is made of flesh, i.e.
it is what I say it is, not merely an image, a trope.
Imagine what a surprise that must have been: a living tongue.
And her gripping half of it, and he gripping the other
half. And the world readjusting all around, as worlds do.

[ST MELANGELL'S DAY, EASTNOR (II)]

The Book of Doves opens to the Chapter of Bridges.
In my youth the most frightening dreams
involved turbid water, something beneath the muddied
surface, something dangerous that remained
unseen. And I was staring down, from a high bank
or some fragile or else broken span. Dream of arches
and of the blind dogs that prowl their stolid footings.
It's time to offer gifts again, to whomever you like.
Because we have lost the Book of Gifts,
from which we might derive more perfect knowledge.
At some point those dreams ceased, for me,
and others took their places, the restless song service
that will never quite begin, the endless queues.
I place the drugs back in their silk sack, I add more salt
to the grinder. Thus do some days carry their ashes
outside, to the clean place. A cycle is restored.
We can be men and women again, though not without
risk. You may read about it in the Book of Tongues.

[ELY CATHEDRAL]

Yes, to all the faces of a person. Yes, to all the scraps. I study walls for
    what grows on or in them. I study clocks in just the same way.
Shadows, though. Shadows study us.
Let's praise the attentiveness of shadows. Let's praise their shadow-
    faces. Their tongues, which don't exist.
The periphery, like a moon, keeps right on singeing, glowing.
A scrap of silence where the factory once stood. What is this thing
    called sound?
I like steel, I heard the man in shirtsleeves say to his friend.
Or, you can buy things all night. Online. In person, at the big-box stores,
    the 24-hour supermarket.
You can buy needles, you can buy framed works of art. The carrion-
    ground's mark set into living stone, the embankment, dark, moist.
I am thinking about the golem in sight of some blossoming pear trees.
    Did it blink. Did it grow a beard, did it reverence the dead. Its
    dead, any dead.
Let's stand guard over the paintings night's jury is mulling. Let's skip
    the execution.
I wrote that we broke into the empty house & told ghost stories there.
    This was a lie. (Or, perhaps this was the ghost.)
Yes to every window. Yes, of course, to bells, & to the ropes from which
    they hang.
Let's ask the sea for its birth sign, its birth stone. We can meet the other
    artists there, we can chant the way the forest taught us.
Yes to the sea, that tries & tries.
On the bookmark I'd scrawled "approach," then "delete," followed by
    some numbers.
Let's teach the sea its numbers. (This will take some time.) Let's wheel
    the sea into the sun, in its special chair.
I woke into stone proofs, dense, mathematical. I thought, death has no
    knowledge of absence.

I stroked the service dog in the hospital corridor. Yes to the service
dog, to the hospital corridor strung with blue icicle lights.

Try to imagine a different war, you suggested.

The smell of photographs lay all over the island like a light jacket, a
fleece. A film of what one person wanted to write.

We are troubled, we plan walks into forests we've read about. Let's
praise the banished radio, muttering to itself in its battered
Quonset.

Yes to strangers, for whom the breath is a dry staple. Let's add water
to the breath, to make it easier to peer through.

The dead shake their flimsy windows at us.

I pointed out, for my students, the various sadnesses of the dead.
Let's build a sea for them, I suggested.

I asked my mother about other men (not my father) she might have
slept with. She wouldn't reply. I asked my father (etc. etc.). He
struck me. "None," he said then, "& if I had, I wouldn't tell
you."

Think about what the golem would have painted, if it had had that
chance. If it had been trained in panting.

Think about memory (without actually remembering).

Our feet softening as we trudged back from the mountain in new
shoes, too perfect.

Let's praise bridges, that bruise the river's soft hair.

I'd wanted to measure the animals but the soldiers prevented me,
slouched in their new uniforms. *Sir*, they kept saying: —*Sir*.

I rubbed & rubbed at my forehead, little cities of teeth visible
through the plate glass of the vast & efficient greenhouses.

The face, though. A precipitation the sea apprehends as a season,
autumn perhaps.

Holiness carries itself past the ruined grist mill, the swans' nesting
site, past the petrol station. That's the physics of holiness: it
carries.

Yes to praise, the soul's milled dentures. It makes the slightest sound,
like an animal licking itself.

[ST MELANGELL'S DAY, EASTNOR (III)]

We lived in the age of explanations, then. We mistook them for light.

And for all our medical needs we were prescribed song: flu-song, contusion-song, cancer-song.

Was it any better or worse this way. Did you hear the stranger knocking.

Doors are remarkable, that we live in a world so full of them. The lack of doors, also remarkable.

We stand inside the calendar of doors & learn to tell time that way, placing our hands on each in turn, feeling for heat, vibration.

Because the dead can't hurt you, or—no more than they already have, not here, not anywhere.

In the fairytale the dead are orphans in some other world, they search for their proper parents among the mannequins & manques.

The math can accommodate this is a sentiment we'll all be tired of hearing very soon. (There is very little math can't accommodate.)

At large in the corridor of objects—kept in from the park by the rain— the children hurtle up & down the scuffed parquet.

I myself learned neither to walk nor talk until I was almost three. I remember bits of that, living without language, or, more accurately, not recognizing the difference between speech & non-speech.

My grandmother, carefully underlining her Christian Science lesson with a blue pencil.

Plato is responsible for many griefs; Christianity as we know it is one of them.

On the other hand, I learned, later, to tune my voice (with others) to overtones. $1 + 1 = 3$.

It was not a bad lesson to learn, among the broken animals.

The itinerant maker of silhouettes snipped at the black paper, glancing up periodically at the shadow my head cast against the canvas dropcloth.

In the framed version, I & my sister's shadows face one another.

In my dream I felt beneath the couch cushions, under the bed for
a missing tooth, which I never found. (All my teeth remained
in place, my tongue confirmed.)

I laced up my boots clumsily, with my left hand only, because my
right was tightly clutching something, something else.

I wiped the mud from my sleeve on the wet grass, gently, like
brushing the crest of some rare bird.

The thing about objects is that they don't mind. The children
crash into them, into one another.

Carefully painted wax organs of the 18th century, come walk with
me. It's late, I know. Come teach me your language of signs.

The city ticking like a vast metronome in the middle distance of
the lithograph.

Promise me you will remember what faith feels like, the lovers
begged, hand in hand at the lintel. I touched my eyelids, my
forehead, my breastbone, my lips.

Did you hear the stranger knocking: no, I did not. Or so I insist,
pretend.

Salt's deep curve disappearing into the mirror's negative space,
goodbye, goodbye.

We hitchhiked through the war, we made our living as jugglers, in
spite of our amputations.

Because even in war-torn countries children wish to see, once
more, gravity defied.

[ST MELANGELL'S DAY, EASTNOR (IV)]

The hill's green sleeve emerging from the mist like some sort of magic trick.
Or like transubstantiation: from earth, from water the body
of a god. From the cries of ewes & lambs. There is a little time left to rescue
the world from the world, & from its denizens.
I clapped my hands once, twice, into the broken city, its porphyry harp.
My face felt the echo as an alphabet, from which it tried to draw some standard
syllable. Meet, face, the chordal horn,
the ancient wood replete again beneath the cuneiform sun. Ash & beech.
I suffer myself to breathe, in the natural manner.
My ribs rehearse their genealogies.
And is not everything perfect, the lilac insists, spreading itself
across each of the five human senses.
Never blame the law for what shadow represents, its prescient discontinuity.
Green sleeve of the hill withdrawing, leaving my arm bare again at dusk.

[ST MELANGELL'S DAY, EASTNOR (V)]

I sat with my back to the forest & its consonants, its fricatives, its glottal stops. Imagine the invitations to the wedding printed on oak leaves; let the wind mail them. The wind's runes are large & intricate. They recognize one another as initiates do, by cowls & stems. Let's watch them nod to one another in May's bare chancel. My nearest living, human friend is sixty miles distant, resting from his accident. So make new friends, the lilac counsels, draft your own mystery play. The lilac doesn't care, but it is mildly interested, as is the nature of lilacs, which spend so much of the vernal year asleep in photosynthesis. They pin their hair back against the storm's messengers, its advance guard. It's not enough to trust in clothing, for sooner or later someone will creep up to any window left glowing through the night. A candle's attention, fragile beneath its god, the moon, to whom it wishes to lend only a little fire, a little wax, a little wick (the moon lacking all these things). I study the economies of medieval illuminations, recurring images: snail versus knight, hare with harp. Each of these was new, once, at least to each other. German, French, Flemish drifting over the hedges, blithe coins. *Never never never* chanted the angels in their tight ring. They whirled faster & faster. Moon, sun, & moon again, small towns, a bass beat, my sister (whom I am not permitted to mention in my poems). Or, how deep the walls extend, beneath the verdured surface. You never know: the body of a child could seem unimaginably heavy or not heavy at all, depending. Each day weighs the same when placed on a scale. Behind me the forest performed its single, slow genuflection. I would never lie to you: I have many friends, & my parents are not yet dead. Select a gate now from the Deck of Gates, tape it to your forehead like a carnival mask. The sheep, agitated by something, rush to the upper pasture. It occurs to me I have never touched a sheep's tongue, living or dead. The tongues of the living are exquisite instruments, not metaphors—not like the members of angels, twelve to each. I contain marrow. This astonishes me. Little factory, come be my bride. We can dwell there, we can watch the sleeping swans. I inferred a currency among the billows of spring rye. Let's spend it. Let's lower the book into the well of cool water. Because even a book can thirst, as it can also demand receipt, standing obdurately at the brass till. That little mirror hanging in the chancel of the ancient, disused church—what was it for? I stepped carefully around it at first, then faced it, confirmed my reflection. It was too small to glimpse the forest behind me. Now I carry the forest on my broad back. It is observant, it is devout, my forest. I break it in two on the footbridge over the river named for my ancestors, who were lighter than I. Perhaps they were birds. Sometimes I think they were birds. Birds of prey, evening hunters, for whom the forest was neither cloak nor trope, but demesne.

[ST MELANGELL'S DAY, EASTNOR (VI)]

Fresh rosemary of the kitchen garden, ride me. Because I want to be ridden, like an alphabet, or a glossary of unfamiliar terms. I whose tongue selects for amnesia, for the scraping of parchments. Not my mind, not my eye, but my tongue. With my fingers I snap off a bit of you, crush you into my palm. The palm is, let's say, a horse. The palm is not subject to any law of sacrifice, only to the mind's will, the tongue's blank dare. So ride the palm. The lilac will teach you (as it taught Whitman, in the midst of another war). False prophet, yes, but prophet nonetheless. I stepped into the kitchen garden by accident, as I do most true things. This much we share, friend rosemary: a god, our ideas about God, towards when we bend, stretch, & break. Ride me as you ride light, the light of these Malvern Hills. It is a light with powers, it can breathe underwater, a light with gills. Amphibious light of the Marches after spring rain measuring the infinite greens, one against the others. Let's compare appetites, distances. Choice is one word for destination, object of motion through time & what we term space. Who accompanies whom on this pilgrimage, this uprising. Translucent scrawls along the river's thigh, can you read them? I can't either. As patterns we circle one another, the burning key. You make no sound that I can distinguish, nor do you dance; you do not know praise. This saves us both some time. Ride me to wherever it is you are going, I don't care. Because I want to be ridden. And because my God—our God—will be there, waiting, when we arrive.

HEPHAESTUS IN NORFOLK
"And all their lifted fingers burned" —*John Masefield*

I walked through fields of wheat, then fields of mustard
clenched like the ear of some sleeper
who is just about to wake, who has in fact woken
but is, for whatever reason, unable or unwilling to move
This is all a paraphrase, a voice whispered
but when I asked "of what?," all I heard was the sky's
low and level drone, that is not about grief
that does not make incisions in the bodies of children
interred, temporarily (as we hope), in the district hospital

In the second part of this poem, I approached
the disused farmhouse, rubbish radiating from it
like spokes from a wheel, I laid first one finger, then two
against the broken latch of the garden gate
beneath me the farm lane was crushed brick, mortar
still clinging to some joints, no idea where it came from

There is no third part to this poem; I left that place

In the myth of Hephaestus, as played by the rabbits
of Edingthorpe, there is a chorus
that imitates the sounds of the hammer, the tongs
in the voices of rabbits, which are rarely used
around men, unless the life of a rabbit is in immediate
danger. I stood in the fog, watching myths
cancel one another out, over and over again, I asked

for a complete and final tally of myths
I wanted a photograph of myth's shriveled foot

I offered my apprentice as a guide to blinded Orion
Don't worry, you'll come back soon, I told him
this was not the first of my lies
broad low tone of East Anglian sky, I am listening

It is true, I wept when informed of language
and when language bore other language, I wept again

beside the mustard fields, in Norfolk in May
snapped violin of the town dormant on the horizon
pulling my tanned and stitched skins
more tightly around my approximate body
while pollen settled, inquisitive, in my brow and beard

I asked the rabbits, do you know any other plays
They scattered into the fields, into the ruined farmhouse
That's two, then, I noted
the play of presence, and then the play of dispersal
in which I am the only remaining witness
I, and the wheat and the mustard, and the scouring sky

[ADDITIONAL EASTNOR POEM (I)]

The forest's glyph unreadable, a besieged city. A letter refused by
   its recipient, & then refused again, in turn, by its author.

Named for (a) the subliminal operations of the human mind, and/
   or (b) the motion a needle, threaded, makes in air, its quick
   dart & thrust.

Earlier we had gazed at the fossils, the ammonites like the script
   of some majestic lost empire.

Permission is one story we tell about this, when we tell stories.

Or the one about the spiral book—you said you dreamed it, it
   was a book, a regular book, except that it took the form of a
   spiral. It wasn't clear how to open it, or turn its pages.

I wanted to take the forest to a hospital, I wanted a doctor's
   opinion. Sessile oak, dying ash.

To make use of something, to manage it for use. This is the
   difference between poetry & drama.

I find it very difficult, I'd confessed, to muster any sympathy or
   empathy for the invertebrates, no matter how necessary
   scientists insist they are.

We were in another country, or planning to go to some other
   country: the same thing, it seemed.

Berlioz crashing from someone else's radio, through the open
   window.

I catalogued & numbered the various smokes as they emerged
   from the plain beyond the ridge.

Under CAST OF CHARACTERS, I read "Skin. Harp. Primelight.
   Consequence." All to be played in the museum. The patrons
   to constitute the chorus.

That endless reticulation, that management of pressure. (Of use.)

I had contacted the museum because I'd discovered, I believed,
   something about one of the artists represented there,
   something no one else knew.

They had sent me to the forest, they had commissioned me with
my water bottle & Claude glass.
Named for the particular dizziness felt when gazing very closely at
a metal surface. Or for an obscure, now lost pigment.
I try to imagine these late medieval men, rubbing the bright gesso
from their altars.
I tried to imagine what the forest had to teach us, this time.
Afflicted forest. Lame forest. Forest of curfewed bells.
I stood in the wings; I was wearing my usual clothes, my pilgrim's
garb. Staff in hand.
Tell me more about the spiral book, I asked, but you would only
shake your head. "I can't describe it more clearly than that,"
you said.
At the banquet, cutlets of meat stewed in chocolate & pomegranate,
served in glittering tureens.
I would bathe the forest, I would cleanse it. (Are you writing this
down, you asked.)
Because what is abandoned—a specific sense of the lover's palm,
or an intimate knowledge of topological functions—can be
re-assembled as a constellation, if the night is long enough.
If the night is not long enough, special instruments are required.
We can't see most stars by day.

[ADDITIONAL EASTNOR POEM (II)]

Winter's antiphon among the hedgerows. I asked my breath to reserve
   a place for me, for us.

If you could create your own grammar, enforce its use among others,
   would you, she asked. By then the rehearsal was underway, & we
   were dressed again in rags.

Rags are sacred objects. They can, like other sacred objects, be washed
   or hidden.

We are traders here, seeking the best bargain, our own best interest.
   The objects we have to vend to one another are all either very
   small, or else very large.

I wiped the sweat from my forehead, my eyes. The body's hollow
   respiration, its bridal theft.

I wanted to describe, fully, subjectively, the science of overtones, only
   without speaking, & without consequence.

I wanted to label each book according to the hours of sleep, that
   fractional pain.

[ADDITIONAL EASTNOR POEM (III)]

But what did it *sound* like, you asked me, later. Winter's antiphon.
  —Like a doll sewn from scraps of calm, I replied.
A doll that could not dance, you persisted. Or would not, I
  responded. (I rather think "would not.")
We were speaking together of familiar things. Of appetites, & the
  pure objects, beech, lens, vellum.
We had agreed that history has no grammar, no melody; it is most
  akin to the medieval drone.
But to be removed from the ceremony because of a *tattoo,* I heard
  the woman in line complain, *a bloody tattoo.*
Where once we smote our breasts in grief, pulled our hair, gashed
  our garments. (Sure, you said.)
Winter genuflects to anything: music, the human pulse, cheese.
  Winter's antiphon is steady. Winter *corresponds.*
There was a war, again, & young men were dying in it. Only they
  no longer wrote poems.
They had traded their eyes for something perfect. What, I asked.
  —What, you echoed.
In the ophthalmologist's office, waiting, trying to count each of my
  teeth with the tip of my tongue, which I had burned earlier
  that day on strong coffee.
That's why it's the lips that should be the author of the oracle, not
  the tongue, you admonished.
The resonant bell of the human skull, its communicating cavities.
  The teeth play their part.
When the provost wrote of "medieval ruins," I responded, "They're
  only 'ruins' if one wants them to be. They can be other
  things, too."
Winter's table, with legs that resemble the haunches & clawed feet
  of wolves. I saw it in the cemetery.

I took photographs of the larger fungi in the forest, some of them
     with a light dusting of snow.
Hildegard wrote, "And in front of her was the figure of a child
     dressed in a pale tunic and white shoes." Also, "like the
     sound of a word and not the actual word itself."
Here, place your hand, feel the residual warmth. Here, place your
     hand, you said: the amputee's stump.
Now, in our postmodern & postcolonial age, we no longer think of
     wars as being *cold.* Or, for that matter, of being conducted
     underground.
The monograph on elm blight lay untouched on the living room
     settee. I placed my sweating glass on it, without thinking.
Letters forming on the surface of the fog, as they also do on the
     surface of the sea. Silence has nothing to do with it.
Winter's bellcote, winter's choir loft, winter's rude guitar. —You're
     just making this up, my friend complained, my other friend.
And then winter shook him like a handkerchief, & he was still.
We laughed in that chapel, after the other couple, so serious, had
     made their slow exit.
My father, in my dream, attempted to stuff a globe into his mouth.
     I couldn't dissuade him. You'll choke, I kept warning him,
     anxiously wringing my hands from across the vast dining
     room.
My body begins to evolve new organs to interact with the frost, to
     sign its treaties.
Otherwise the restaurant only served bones, some small, some
     large, some blunt, some delicate. Whatever you ordered, you
     were likely to receive a bone, on a plate.
Empires came & went in precisely this way, of course. (Your broad
     sneer almost trembling.)
Snow was falling, snow was drifting idly among the hedgerows.
     I was clicking through images of bugloss on the internet,
     those deep blues.

Upon learning, at the age of 5, that there was such a thing as cursive writing, I insisted there must also be cursive numbers. I invented some, taught them to the other children. Was punished for that.

Tell me more about your childhood, the war murmurs, trying to place its mutilated hand on mine.

Whether the quantity of the living is greater than all those who have gone before, whether the blue you see is the same blue I see.

Winter parts its own garments among us, it doesn't wait for the soldiers. (So slow, soldiers.)

That door led to the sacristy, those to the chapels in the transepts, all in ruins by the Reformation.

So let's agree, for a moment, that stone is winter's dialect, gravel winter's low immersive chant.

I placed my feet carefully along the remaining planks of the footbridge, rimed in both ivy & ice.

Did the doll have a mouth, you asked. A painted-on mouth, an embroidered mouth, any mouth. (But if I say yes, you'll only ask again: about its teeth, its tongue.)

In its hand it held a wheel, is what I told you, then.

Yes, that is what I am saying. I want to affirm this, now that it's too late. Winter sounded like a doll sewn from scraps, holding a wheel.

[ADDITIONAL EASTNOR POEM (IV)]

Depth of scale, the young lilac blazing in the footlights of the old. Fold the soul this way, that, your Rorschach origami. Crease its neck, flank, torso, wings. Also, the complicity of art. Stars, crease here, fold there, for we are small. I consulted the hospital guidebook, which was printed in seven languages. Gratitude stems from an awareness that the body, as a body, could be somewhere else. Like teleporting accidentally into a clear block of glass, is how she described her death. I let myself into & then out of the deserted villa, trying each key in turn. We are indeed so very small. As you can see, from the aerial photographs. I promised myself no longer to talk to animals, no longer to deny my status as tourist. Depth of scale, the celandine swollen against the appetites of light. So did the Venetians paint that, you asked. A chancel arch, an aumbry. Bread, wine, honey. I stood again with my left hand on the iron balustrade. I could make out, in the distance, some idea of distance. Place the body in the photograph, leave it there. Armies seek the smallest mirror. Sometimes they smash it, sometimes they pass through. Could you remember the quality of shadow in that "holy place," if offered sufficient inducements. Store it in the *tongue,* I thought I heard you say. Lilac fosters lilac, foliate choirs lifted to the water vapor. Fold here, pinch there, my arthritic spine. The logic of the Transfiguration figured not this time in terms of light, but in terms of sleep. The heralds cross their strong arms. I have passed every test I recognized, left it behind in the muddy track. The body's passage through time & space as a cult of *possession:* it leaves a residue. I broke off a sprig of fresh rosemary for no other reason than I wanted to. (See: wanting to.) The wooden throne accommodated me, as it had so many others. There is nothing intrinsically sacred about wings, archaeologists insist. (I stood with them in the field, I recorded their badges.) About the complicity of art: I fell in love with love, once. I drew it up from its dark well. No ideas but in the elements: brass, tungsten, harp, lungs. This is why we are permitted to walk here, the docent explained, gesturing grandly. I noticed the condition of her hair, a winter's seed. Carruth accused late Levertov of trafficking exclusively in emblems. I keep repeating that word, *emblem emblem emblem,* as if it might mean something—something else. Because *motive* is not the past participle of *song.* I left my garments on the heavy, pitted hook provided, my hat & cloak. Skin registers the gravity of stars, somehow. What often happens next is that, lost, we think we don't know where we are. I slipped into the sacristy to view the archived portraits of the dead. Later a woman stopped me on the bridge. I saw you earlier, she told me. Are you an actor, she asked. She had just taught her young son to tell time. She had moved her lips but could not hear the sound. Bodies are like this, traces of evidence left strewn about fields of meat. That we can even say so is prophecy. Here, help me lift this stone, that fell from the sky, that sets the Geiger counters clacking. My accent shifted perceptibly as I walked from one end of that town to another. It is time, I said, to close the book, the only book. We will save the fire sermon for later, little brother.

[ADDITIONAL EASTNOR POEM (V)]
for John Lane

On Elbow Cay, it's easier to consider the pastoral, because the
   detritus between Nature & culture still has a pleasant ratio,
   is what my friend wrote to me.
I looked up into the radioactivity of the heavens, what we call the
   heavens.
It had been an hour since I last touched a living organism, that I
   was aware of.
The little clocks of the body keep chiming, sometimes in sync. I let
   the gnawed core of my pear fall into the bracken.
Heat lightning, vis-a-vis the economies of blame. Paint this, paint
   it now (I told my students).
(But sir, we are not, or no longer, painters.)
The image creeps upon us, often at night, sometimes when we are
   sleeping. Sometimes not.
She had, she told me, "a real problem" with fables. For instance,
   how does one know when one fable is over, & another
   begins.
Jeffers in his round tower above the sea, cloistered with his error.
The job that made my college roommate's career was to record
   sounds in unique acoustic spaces, then construct algorithms
   to imitate them.
I recognize the cup from which I drank last night. Insects crowd
   around it, all wanting their turn.
Say what you will about choice, & theophany will echo it back to
   you, just like in the dream.
Because anything can be made to induce value.
In my dream I was a trained forensic photographer. I photographed
   numbers, exclusively.

The sea is the receptacle for all our wars & brings them back
to us, faithful retainer (is what I wrote in response, to my
friend).

I acknowledge the faces of animals when I eat them. I've read their
sacred books.

He asked me who had built that wall, the monks, or those who
came after the monks. Yes, I replied.

We occupied the guesthouse. We deployed its astrolabe.

The detached head of the capercaillie on the gravel track, gash of
vermilion attended by flies.

I threw my medals into the fire, over & over again.

It began to rain in six old & eleven new languages, simultaneously.

Internally & externally, the same key fits this lock. I don't know
whether I'm going or coming.

I have always admired water's symmetry. (Because you have to
believe in something.)

Photographing the storm & then the lack of storm, my friend's
wife forgot about the banquet.

Some things are actual, i.e. the opposite of naming, of names.

The coast curves & recurves like an idea waiting to be born:
naphtha, radio, the color mauve, the Mass.

I care most about those who lie beyond my field of vision. How
will they eat, where will they sleep.

Little blood-borne tide of salt & prescience, completion's forecast.
It rides the swells.

And I turned then, in the garden, to where the child lay on the
grass, crying, calling for its mother.

Experience is like a lid, is what I thought then.

The wound on my face is not a "feeling." I lift my hand to it, we
have come so far, I have the assistance of mirrors.

[ADDITIONAL EASTNOR POEM (VI)]
Eastnor Castle

I tour the mansion with the children on holiday, I notice the titles
of the books piled on desks, on settees, behind the velvet
ropes.

These things are real to somebody, not necessarily me. (The same
goes for the children, & their parents counting back the
minutes, all but audibly.)

I pause, often at the taxidermied bodies of animals encased in
glass. An owl, a leopard, a capercaillie. None of these things
are messages I'd been intending to open, but hadn't.

The disenchantment with which my friend was preoccupied
settled on us like a bright wheat. Look, I said, that's the
sound rowing makes.

I dreamed we were required to breathe on a vibrating piece of
clear glass, each in turn.

Because some things can't be gainsaid, rainshower at noon, the
tanned leather with which I've chosen to bind the soles of
my feet.

The diagnosis was, as expected, desperate. We did not attend the
final dance performance.

Pugin was, so the story goes, under the impression he was
designing a salon for an actual medieval castle. (See: Roman
Catholicism, fallacies appertaining to.)

An entire monograph could be written on the bell-pulley system
once ubiquitous in English country houses, as on the desire
to float, weightlessly, in space.

She showed me her amateur photographs of planets, taken
through her husband's telescope.

I take a seat in the garden & think, for a time, about penance. Or,
I let penance think about me.

Penance, it seems, is like the exercise when one imagines placing

one's hands into each of Christ's wounds, only carrying
through with it. Wound by wound.

In the private chapel, which is not ancient (though furnished to
appear so), I keep looking around for a Catherine wheel.

Back in town I made sure not to touch the shopkeeper's palm or
wrist as I let the coins fall into her grasp.

Water is about waiting, yes, but also about light, weight, volume.
In this water is like poetry. Glide of a heron afflicting the
surface of the man-made lake.

I tried to photograph the moon's tidal operation on those waters,
but I failed. There was too little water, & my camera was
crude.

This is not my poem, though I do appear in it, faithfully. (We are
never going to be any more faithful than we are now, etc.)

Some things are not, in the end, questions of light, but questions
of blame. We lean into them. Trained surgeons lift our
negligence from our bodies, cut by cut.

Pugin sought a renewed sense of spiritual community through
architecture, in keeping, more or less, with Levertov's
contention (vis-a-vis Duncan) that form is never more nor
less than a revelation of content.

In my dream I pour a second glass of wine, as if I were expecting
someone. Someone else, I mean.

What I was most sorry for was frightening the custodian when I
slipped into the back of the church, wanting, like Mary, to
see where again they had laid the dead.

[ADDITIONAL EASTNOR POEM (VII)]

Thunder must have a hygiene
I emptied the last milk from the bottle, into my mouth
Rinsed the bottle, came that much closer
To immanence
That much closer to the lilac bough
The reliquary, dented & tarnished, was disappointing
We'd had to ask to see it
We'd had to request an audience with the sea
Detached head of the mauled capercaillie by the track
Vermilion head of the dispatched capercaillie
A communion that takes place in the eye
But is not of the eye
To which the eye is merely witness
A signatory, as to some will or deed, a transfer
Two hikers passed me on the path, then two cyclists
Their garments almost exactly the same
Earlier I'd plunged my hand into the heated basin
The wild aurora above my dream-village
Flickering off & on, on & off
I have never, to my knowledge, dreamed of flies
I rinsed the bottle, placed it on the lit sill to dry
Matter murmurs into matter
Like the music of harps, a constant tightening, a key
Possession is nine-tenths of history, my friend
Admonished, from Alaska
Having been, as I note here, a student of possession
I lifted the smell of my own body in both hands
As if it were heavy
As if the ritual, like a garden, required tending
The bonfires, appearing in the distance, frightened me
They burned mauve in the dusk

I shaved my upper lip again, as per custom
Acquired from our time in one of many wasted plains
We are reluctant to relinquish it
We pay the same prices in the stores that you do
What remains unaddressed (in this poem)
Is music, the problem of music
Which is not the same as the problem of fatherhood
Some men manage both, simultaneously
I admire those men
One visited the disused chapel yesterday
While I, unbeknownst to him or to his wife, paused
Behind a screen
He sung a few lines of an ancient hymn, for his wife
That's one I learned on the island, he told her
Soon they strolled away (as did I, tactfully, a bit later)
Of all the things I could have left there
I wanted a shell, from the sea, but I had no shell
It has been many years now since I walked by the sea
I would not describe myself as unhappy
Only devastated
The unbroken vastness of the ear
Represented perfectly by that painter on canvas
Twilight tones, he called them
He had trekked that spring from town to northern town
Keeping a diary as a pledge against sleep
His canvases were another matter, those he sold
In the little markets as in the great houses
Where his friends introduced him (to their friends)
Now we have his versions
Of a horse's head, a lilac bough
Of milk, of a dune, of a copse in the midst of a storm
Wild with lightning (& with his emblem of lightning)
Rendered in his hand
With which it is said he once saved a child
From drowning, or was it a fire, no one is quite sure

[ADDITIONAL EASTNOR POEM (VIII)]

The epigraph was from Hegel, I recognized
God returned His glass eye to me
I was glad; I had coveted it, had missed it
I went through the usual motions, e.g.
Renewing my passport, shopping for figs
I considered the advantages & disadvantages
Of the mute, as a natural class
Hildegard to Provost Andrew of Averbode:
"The secret light says: You are frightened
Of the wind; you are falling asleep
In the green tree of your mind"
I was drowsing in the green tree of my mind
I had missed the slightly inturned path
As it led off through the unripe barley
I retraced my steps
Being a beast & no more than a beast
In possession, now, of the glass eye of God
Its meat-like provender
Its cold & temporizing fire
Of which I had also read, once, in chronicles
Studying the ancient woodcuts closely
The unfamiliar shapes of letters
Hazarding their crude Latin, oblivious
To the snow borne inside our modern guns
This is how I fell asleep, in that distant place
This is how I exchanged my breath
For the complete cartulary of breaths
With its forged charters & inks of iron gall
The men, then, would have drunk milk
Just as I have drunk milk

In the slight shadow of dusk's headland
Its lower slopes burring with hawthorn, ash
All drawn into the eye of God
And then expelled, in proper sequence
Such a fearful thing, this eye of God
Which I am still holding in my sweaty hand
It's with the other hand I write this
Having sold nothing of value to the republic
Having exchanged no signet
With the actual, nor with the actual's decay

[ADDITIONAL EASTNOR POEM (IX)]

Let's break the camera's coal, you said to me
I leaned back against planes
Of brute experience
I'd inherited, as from some father's father
We were friends, you see, the winds knew us
I almost knew your other name
Though within our maculate soliloquies
We often approached the sacred
As through a succession of enameled plates
Chladni had the right idea
Induce a vibration, watch where dust settles
Watch where the gold burns itself into the sea
Of thinking, of names
We were guests at the execution, we bore
Our invitations in the notches of each right ear
Such splendid pageantry
When the corpse leapt up, duly dampened
Let's break that corpse, you said to me
But I pretended I hadn't heard
I pretended I had known capitalism's precincts
I pulled my garment more tightly around
My head
This was all not so long ago
We had both studied, we had both assisted
The prisoners
With their broths & gruels
What then can be said of the heart, the muscle
Whose fist, like a low-slung island
Punches again & again at the gilded thorn
Let's consult the witnesses, you said, & then
I nodded, I consented

I agreed:
Truly, let us go, let us consult the witnesses
Not realizing you were speaking of ourselves
The ruins we had fostered
The silks we had touched, & stained
Being held for us now in all the best museums
Profane veronicas
I can't even begin to describe
What the water felt like, when my body hit
In full view of the cameras of earth, fire, & air

[ADDITIONAL EASTNOR POEM (X)]

*

Long light of the northern sky, stand by my bed
I have no other use for you
I shake my phylacteries in your thousand faces
You lave my limbs with your thousand tongues

HANSEN'S DISEASE

We no longer use the word *jilt.* There is no longer a bank in every town. But you can still reach out, feel the texture of these ancient walls. We await further updates from the field, the virtual expanse. Identity as a word or words chosen, in part, by the eye. Or by the ear. I laid out my debts on the long, low table so that the blind could touch each, individually. How does it feel to be a blind soldier, the journalist asked, and: what is cruelty. The fields were stippled with silence again. Church of silence, I pass you in the street, I nod in recognition to your masked visage. I drew blood from the river's assembled currents, & from their shadows. Let's move now with the rhythms of devotion, mammal-bodies, mammal-echoes in the garden at night. The novel warned us of this, drinking slowly from its cracked cup. Wedding as a measure of distance, not Cana but Gethsemane, in sight of no ocean. I sketched the plaster statuettes huddled on their scrubby mountain slope. I arrived in the city with bruised ribs, a sore in my scalp. I had paid language's bill, played all its waiting games. The waking dreams copy the dreams of the dead, however imperfectly. There they are, hiding among the frescoes. I, myself, have only ever dreamt of one poet, & one king. It was June, all the lights were on, glistening. You put away your paints. The war is forever mourning the sound of its name, which it has forgotten. The white hairs, the pale fire. I wash my clothes again. Or, the seedy prismatics of the park bench. The wax mouth of plenitude, opening. Oscillation of pigments in the tongues of the blind. Music's cool rest, repeated. Applaud wildly, carpenters, my friends, my friends. Brush the ships from your blue sleeve, keep the door closed.

AFTER THE ABOLITION OF FESTIVALS

Let's let the ladder speak. Let's inquire of its country, its citizenship. Let's listen to the ladder's staccato hymn. Mark the calendar, cast the stone into deep water. The dead envy music. Of this much I am sure. Certainly you may visit the garden unmasked. Let's surprise charity in the night, let's wake him up. For he resteth on a palanquin of mute suns. For his epaulettes are all the hues of autumn. If we wake him, perhaps he will walk in the park with us. Photograph the rain's epilogue, if you can. Let's compile a syllabary of ladders. Are you listening, friend. The soldiers also have access to the garden at night. You can't know experience from the other cutlery arranged across the table. The folklore of ladders is very rich, you assured me. Of pious cities. Of the spiritual lives of beasts & bone. Of what happens when the palace burns. Where now will the children sleep? This is an invitation, tendered as currency. So many are afraid of the garden at night. The ember days are upon us, scabbed lions of dusk. We have tattooed their orphans. We have catalogued their saints. Look, I carry my book into the rogue wave. Let's be a waking instrument, let's climb through the paralytic merchant's grate to where he keeps his lambs. These are the lambs of night, the ladder's lambs. It's true, their many-lidded eyes are disconcerting, as is the feel of their tongues. This is the world our father described to us, an arras of smoke. It isn't far now, & it won't be long. Let's balance ladders on our shoulders while we sing, let's pose for the painting. We can sing anything. We are strong like chemicals. Let's worship what the ladders worship. Let's start now.

THE EARLIEST WITNESSES

Let us write, then, the glistening poem.
Body of the polyphemus moth
softening against the drizzle's grain—
it has no voice
it is the antithesis of voice.
I am a thing of voice, bent low
over the voiceless, studying
it, gauging it against what I once knew.
Droplets like little pearls
against its scale-shedding wings.
Of what great price are we constructed,
master of calamities, what commitments
to unattended islands.
I am not in the least
tempted to weeping. There is a time
for weeping,
just as there is a time for glass.
The lovers pass the Regency mirror
without pausing, without gazing
into its depths. The platform
on the jubilee bridge seemed unserious,
perfunctory, a flip concession.
What is permanent
versus what is splendor
is what the war is counting out, now,
in pawnlight's chronic dysphasia.
Oculi, things that look like eyes,
that remind the eyed observer of itself.
Later, we will study the reflections,

each carefully sealed
inside the wing of some godlike being.
I prod it with a stick. I am shameless.
We have such trouble
photographing the brides
as they procession from the dark hall.

[THE LINE, ITS SLEEK ARK. STOW]

The line, its sleek ark. Stow the creatures where the calendar
can't snatch them. Coal is unreasonable in all its phases.
Into the open *pearls,* I was, at first, sure I'd read. The coasts of it,
vast hythes of what is generally regarded as pleasure. Gnosticism,
its thick deictic hull. The line tendered above the chapel
& such periphrastic floods. I want, she said, you to see the light
on this particular hill. (This was later.) So I queued to experience.
Prayer glossed in & out, a brute lacquer. Tell me
not what you want but what the line measures: the wingspans
of ravens or doves; Judaism; the etymology of *entity,*
condensed on the cool glass pane. Did you find it in the avenue,
did you just take it. The risks of months, their thin leaves
superimposed. One hides another. There was a great glow
there, she said, gesturing precisely into where oxygen had been.
And say a student proposes, not justice, but *the just,*
at the moment the siren pierces the street's dowsing monosyllable.
You would have admired the wildflowers too. The psychology
of doors, aberrations of (*q.v.*). I woke to the gardener
rapping on the bedroom window. Let's press some riddling prime,
smooth the holiday's gay chains. Because here we are together
beneath the brass key of rain, a thousand sacred
assignations. What is *just* about a plate, a mesh, music's inclined
plane. I wanted a space filled entirely with not-me, not-us.
It could have been an ocean. Abusive striations
of the inevitable, such versets. O antigen. We have drunk again
from purpose. We have met fire's strangest ode. I felt the lamb's
ears first, yes. Only then did I stroke its breathless eye.

[LLANDYFEISANT CHURCH (I)]

Consider myself a rival, consider myself arrived. Small life
knows this place, its nooks & swells. Trouble the grasses, trouble the stone.
Men placed stones here: this much is certain. Sun knows it, moon
knows it, pale-fly, angleworm. Christ knows & is known.
The Christ of stone, of the lizard's broad back. Inhume vs. subsume.
No space is "abandoned," "disused." Rood of the locked door, the sealed
porch. Oh gardener I have surprised you on your lunch break,
your tools silent, your shirt off. You hurry away. There is no mistaking
blood for anything else, nothing else bears the pulse's thread.
I tie it around my tongue, around a twig of yew. These latter days
of canceled amplitudes. Row with them, out to the useful place, the used
place. I will not meet you there. Some things are built to fall into ruin—
Faith is one. The body is another. Stunned credit of the swallow's veer,
the osprey's swoop. What does "regard" mean, anyway. Observe:
the true nations disgorge their shy beasts, they give them up. *Abducto,*
to lead away. I will be right here, tool or tooth. I dreamt of pain
& then woke into it, a whir of orange wings. Is there something else
that might be done, the concierge asked, solicitously. Her first language
was not my first language, & we both knew this, animals among
the other animals. But my first language was silence. I learned to read
before I knew to speak. Perhaps that was best. Squall
of avian bargaining, the understory, the canopy prevenient in Welsh
light. I wrap my arms around a stone & am not ashamed, or only
a little. The garret-fly samples my oils, my sweat. I am a creature of images
towards which the world, like any world, turns. Turns, & vanishes.

CASTLE WOODS, DINEFWR

Most things have hidden roots, why not piety, that crow's wing.
I bought a card at the shop, mailed it to my brother.
He asked nothing of me. Did you imagine some greater riddle,
then. A spindle-whorl. A spool. Dog-rose in flower at the Tywi's
edge. You may make an image if you like. The sheep do it.
Ants do it in and through their labors, their chemical mazes.
It is time, my friend said, to reckon our exhaustion, to tote it up.
That is, after all, what math is for, its foolproof schematic.
Dig deep into the eye, the saints advise. They remember time
but no longer understand it. I remember
the single crow drinking from the ancient well, that startled
as I drew near. This happened in time, its plague of roots
undermining every present motive. Here are some things
other people do inside buildings, give or take a thousand years—
is what I wrote my friend. The dedicated space
inside the chancel was very small. Whether to construct
a larger chancel was debated, then rejected. Because,
it was argued, the dead lie sleeping there, in their natural forms.
It is easy to forgive measure: the wild garlic, the devastated
bluebells in the wood. My bruised ribs seek a shelter—
other than the body, I mean. Once, I talked in my sleep.
Now I watch workmen clear the failed plantation of everything
that resembles glass. I count, as every beast must, the flecks
of ash that fall upon my pelt. I was surprised, my teacher-
friend confessed, by how few children knew the name of that
old war. I am surprised by dog's mercury, pink campion,
bird's-nest fern at the path's clean edge. You can draw a town
on any map. Imagine the people who live there, what they stow
in their gardens, their medical anomalies, their sports teams.
Just the same we are never very far from an altar, here.
One can be very precise about worship, about the intensity

of the sun and other light that travels further to rest
within our cells, to mimic rest. The family arguing in Welsh
is not part of the permanent display, the docent clarified.
Remember the children's inflatable birthday pavilion
stripped of its gaudy hexachords. Perceptible matter goes a long
way towards explaining the universe, but never far enough.
That is why mammals engage in breath, ceramics, politics.
We are all guests at the Festival of the Senses:
some of us blindfolded, some of us the dispensers of blindfolds.
No one comes here to the lichen throne (which seats four)
except the aging groundsmen with their scythes.
Their tattoos remind them of other, distant loyalties, past loves.
As do mine, but mine are all, in the conventional sense, scars.

[DINEFWR CASTLE (II)]

Let the phrase build. Milk's royal sephirot, its tissue-tree. Had I been taken here as a child I would be no different. But not some tragic candle, abandoned at the altar. Welsh light in the selvage, illuminating the knoll's dim pledge. Some consonants carry further than others. This might matter, say, in a guerilla scenario, or at the end of the world. Lift the embroidered cloth from the marriage feast; lift it with great care. The forecast calls for light war, war in the morning clearing in the afternoon, 40% chance of war. I measured out a length of bone, called it a psalm. Now I am Sebastianed with psalms. They've drawn my voice from its dank well, tried to gild it. But the blood resists all ornament, unlike the flesh, unlike bone, the frightened syllabaries of the merely fluent. Rejoice, for today is the festival of blood, & flesh, & bone. You may wear your special hat, or other priestly headgear. You may pass once, twice, through the fire, which we have equipped with mechanical angels, latest working models. Partly war, partly milk, partly faith collecting in the cisterns, the shallow catchments. The cries of the disinherited reach us even here, across the green plain, the carriageway's Dopplered curve. What are the language arts, my mother asked. I brushed an ant from her sleeve. But I want to *know,* she insisted. Together we walked through that forest, pulling limbs & branches to one side. The procession swerves by word of mouth, by flag of tongue. Raw negligence. I have no proper guardian, in the event of language, in the event of war. I mortar every brick with milk, blood, lymph, semen, bile. At last we removed the broken wreath from the gate. A bird had nested in it, or tried to. Welsh light permeating motive, doctrine, greeting: a northern light, but not hard like cold panes, & never frangible. The word I want to teach the flesh today is *restraint.* I tutor its branches, I catechize its roots. The flesh's alphabet, derived from its own organs, is capable of great literature, & also treachery. Equally subject to pressure, severance, decay, & flame.

[DRYSLWYN]

The sheep are built of glass, metal, stone. They move so slowly.
They do not, in any conventional way, burn.
The end of the world as a gothic arch, with nothing on the other
side. Absolute nothing, zero-dimensional.
This is a false statement of the problem, because it lies about
the nature of God. And yet we see ourselves compressed,
reflected, in that point.
Cue the sheep's midnight pyre. They have witnessed nations.
Their eyes tutor the hawthorn, the elderflower.
Rustle of my bootsteps among the winding grasses, their jubilant
treasuries of sugar, light, & earth. They neither lift nor are
they veil. Nettle, campion.
But what are angels' tongues made of, I heard the child ask its
mother, in the dingy shop. (They are made either of bread
or of glass, or of the end of the world.)
Flatbed after flatbed of molded concrete bridge abutments
heading south, that is, away from this place. A kestrel rides
the thermals.
Feast of twine, feast of immaculate forgetting.
The earth is a prodigy & I am its house, I tell the children, arrayed
around me in my dream. On their haunches, damp with
drizzle.
We wake into math, sometimes gently, more often abruptly. We
think math is a cruel master, but this, too, is error.
I make a list of what has gone missing from this place, & then I
cross it out. Sing, my bruised rib commands.
Damage's sole memory, often constructed, is of not-damage. From
these two poles, the triangulation of experience.
Bone, I hiss at the sheep. They thrash & quiver. Their eyes roll,
slowly, on their slender eyestalks. They hum, low & in
unison.

Perhaps these are not sheep. (But, the end of the world—etc.)

No one is interested anymore in the poem as a scrim, as something light passes through, by design. I press my pen against my thigh.

Let's clothe the narrow places with silk, while we have time, while we have silk. Parliament of the notochord, dismissed.

I go on touching the elder, the ash, the sycamore with my weak-twinned gaze. Let's think about thirst together.

That math allows for both bread & flight is simply astonishing. (The hazel, the beech, the cedar, the oak. The ash again.)

I lay my head on the hill's steep slope. *Depend* in the punitive sense.

The very tall man said, at some point you cease to be beautiful, you are merely a freak. Can this be said of landscape. (The stone lambs, the glass lambs.)

I measure the math with my calipers, I trim it faithfully with my small sharp knife, I pare it back.

What we don't know is where, if anywhere, they buried their dead. (Beneath their living, I would expect you to offer, drily.)

Would you call what you do *wandering,* the gardener asked.

Ruin is tenable, it's not just a recitation of forms. I grasp it, wrote Averroes. We are deep into the default of love, & love's parenthesis.

Gray, green, & blue, the emblems run. (The sheep recognize this, pull tightly to the center of their demesne.)

Pity's rapid posture, at the mouth of the great net. The lambs with their heads full of eyes, studded with eyes, streaked & tacky pearls.

It means the same thing, my teacher told me, after the accident. Not ungently.

[LLANDEILO CHURCHYARD (I)]

When I went to visit the holy well I found a little child there. He
was texting on his phone. He didn't look up.

Water lifting water, read the plaque by the estate pump-house.

So much of my life has been spent in postures of waiting. (What
literature & faith hold in common.)

Radiant expectation, the yew's gathered cloths, the elm's crippled
homage.

We are all invited to the Festival of the Senses. Some blindfolded,
some as vendors of blindfolds.

Both waking & sleeping I study lichens. I know more about them
in my dreams than in waking life.

The mowers again, this time in their Welsh masks, their festival
masks. I doff my hat & step aside.

Blue light of the iPhone in the holy well's dank recess. I make
nothing up, I assure you.

I kept walking down that ancient street. Somewhere nearby, a
local band covering CCR (badly, but with conviction).

Thirst says, You could have a drink, if you wanted to.

Devotional space, water's volume function. Open the book, close
it, open it again.

Is the book about pain, you ask. That's a good question, I reply.
(All questions are good, you insist.)

The ford, the ram, alluvial drift. Oxbows of the flood plain, faith's
water cycle.

I watched from the terrace as the older man unloaded his cases of
soda, his bottled juices.

You could buy gold here, or silver. Musical instruments
handcrafted with artisanal care. Fabulous garments (the
end of the world, etc.).

The police presence glistening like a droplet on skin. I don't
necessarily mean human skin.

Drink this. It's on the dead, on the house (of the dead).

I recall being able to hit a high C with a purity of tone that made others jealous (& this frightened me, a little).

In those masses loosely classified as "parodies," pressing the secular for its spangled plasma.

The yew as centrifuge, hurling everything it is & isn't toward its periphery. (Don't think they're blind, the old woman warned me.)

A celebrity promises to swim the Great Pacific Garbage Patch. "Mind over matter," he intones.

I've made only two vows in my life. I broke one.

Heal the scalpel, heal the center's variant refrain.

At the Festival of the Senses, booths for eating, listening, touching. I lead the blind with a long, knotted rope.

Or, sometimes, music's faint meniscus, resting on something else: a voice, a stone, these Bartlett pears.

The boy did not look up at me, or into the water. What was he there for, then. Streaks of old coal at the cornice.

Maybe the book is about pain—since it flows through my hands. (This is in my dream. Because while I do look, I don't actually touch the water, don't let it touch me.)

Beside the basin, a damaged photograph, some wilted blossoms, something the field coughed up: asters, forget-me-nots.

A child's idea (gazing into his phone, his pale face lit with the blue light).

When I say the word "filter" to myself, over & over again, it begins to sound like an organ of the body, something bruisable. Excisable.

The variant refrain, the luminous white cloth.

If you were an image would you wash or be washed. Would you have that choice.

I tip the wineglass over. Fortunately, it's empty.

I believe in neither ghosts nor mirrors, but am visited by both. They leave a pale residue as evidence of their passage.

The little train clanking past, Ffairfach, Llandybie, Ammanford.
  Swansea, eventually.

Aesthesia, affliction. To touch the *gods,* I thought I read.

Perhaps that is what the boy was doing, or thought he was doing,
  in the presence of water.

We will attend the pantomime another evening. From a distance,
  the sound of some mammal, crying.

[LLANDEILO CHURCHYARD (II)]

The church, like a bubble, is iridescent & very thin, very fragile. We try to teach it language, our language.

In the distance, nuclear power plants, sheep.

Like a bubble, like a stretch of glass, the church understands gravity, but not quantity. It worships the dog-rose, a bit.

I wrote myself into the allegory in the form of an open door.

The life-sized papier-mâché mannequins at the reconstruction were terrifying. Was this intentional?

We were allowed to touch the velveted walls of that empty house, the period wallpaper.

Inside the soap bubble that is the church lies a single, perfect tooth.

I want the church to make a noise, to speak or sing, shout or murmur—but it doesn't.

Imagine it as lamplight. Imagine it as a child's initials, carved into an honest bench.

I asked myself, is this a church, is this what a church looks like. I counted my remaining teeth, each sidereal emperor.

Because it serves the interests of power to relate the simplest explanations, the ones, for example, that feature talking animals in lieu of graves.

During the renovation, the pilgrim's preserved shoes were misplaced, or else stolen. I saw the leather & embroidery of the replicas in a photograph.

Thousands of churches floating across the park, into the dog-rose, into the hedge, each with its tooth. (The deaf, the dumb, the blind, the lame, etc.)

Now you have lost your glasses. No one will talk to you.

Let's study the celestial charts together, I want to say (to the good-looking young couple with their perfect baby).

Let's abandon the security of the subjunctive, that hums like a hive.

Cars drive right through the center of the dead, without seeing them. People in their cars, listening to their radios.

Rook in the cedar, which the church recognizes, vaguely. Bright annulus of the sycamore's host, immaculate.

Tell the makers of fables to lay down their adzes.

Pain knows its own song, which it teaches to the body, stubborn child, a hammer's breath.

The *hand*written, that undersoul. (Is what I thought you'd written.)

We had parked at the edge of the field at dusk, as if awaiting someone, someone else.

Little organs of the body, there is no such thing as a hidden war. I am almost done being a tourist here.

Sometimes a tooth is just a key, you told me.

I first wrote *guilty* alibi, then *prodigal* alibi. As if I were speaking into the tooth. As if the tooth were an ear, a human ear.

The church only knows one name, the name of a city. This I learned in my years as a guard, & as a friend to guards. It is not & was never your name.

[CARN GOCH]

Friend oxygen, I strip your creche, now it lies despoiled in the long
    light, the northern light.
This is the finest place, from which to watch the lives of others.
I am trying to understand something very, very large & yet enclosed,
    bounded. (That is, not God.)
In the red city I worked as an agent for a manufacturer of hooks.
    Models hung from my leather vest; I jangled when I walked.
Math feels very personal here, & physics, contact sports into which
    we're drafted.
One almost feels one could eat stones.
Invisible beings play their part in economies of value, that production
    process. (See: faith's water cycle, disarrangement of.)
I sit with my back to the ancient town, the saint's hermitage, the
    Kuznan takeaway.
Remember boldly the unexplained phenomena, the Fortean husks.
You would not be surprised by anything here, by design. Sleeplessness,
    the same sort of exposed promontory with its sheaves & musks.
White noise of a distant jet, wind, some saints' pulses emigrating, etc.
You are a brilliant star running parallel to mercy's page.
Now everything is available but nothing is known. The lichens I sit on
    may be hundreds of years old.
I wore my lightest, brightest shirt to the birthday celebration. I can't
    believe in mirrors here, can't even imagine.
Where the dead store their water is another question.
Athwart language the eye falters, turns inward, recites again the same
    menu choices.
She said, This place has not known Christ. —Now it has.
But if the saints had passed through it, in their long queues, their
    ragged robes. One end to the other, little flames.
For flame is the glory of bone, just as bone is the glory of breath.

To feel simultaneously *suspended & upheld.*

I have no one to share this place with but you, friend oxygen, friend thief.

Drink, then, last captain of the reconnaissance. Dedicate every guest, to the extension of guests.

There are no clocks here. I, a clockmaker, am both free & stung.

The Desert Mothers would have understood, would have gotten this exactly right, the silence. (The Desert Fathers would have robbed the stones to build their cells.)

In the end everything is rendered magnificently intangible. This is the logic of the Mass.

Here I feel only the lack of my love for God, whom I love. Here in the melisma of absolutes.

Make haste, friend, to solve the equation of iron. (And its brutal kings? Yes, its brutal kings.)

You will pass through a slow wreath of psalm-light.

You may go anywhere you want, where other animals have gone. (See, their brailled traces, their broken, discarded bells.)

The cathedral was entirely empty except for me, I mean my body.

I moved carefully, at the edge of God's stealth.

The great forms condescend to us. They bring new smells with them, the smell of fresh snow, for example, or the bright patois of mint.

I walked in that place with the war overhead, a caul. I felt at perfect peace, then recalled, for a moment, the Armenian genocide. All those empty masks.

Water lifting water, blood lifting blood.

The stone anthem, that I learned in my dream—& woke, later, humming.

Is not the hair of graves, partisan: you are mistaken. (I never want to bring a student here, to stoop to explanation.)

You could bleed here, if you wanted to, you could shed your blood. Would that change anything?

These are the generations of stones, the stones in their generations.

(What must this hillside be like when nothing cries out.)

Abrade them softly, with the hands, as one would a lump of clay, or dough.

The cathedral of ribs, so bright & empty now. I mean, of our motives.

That was one of the most beautiful films I have ever seen, she told me.

(We were in the nearly-closed restaurant, after.)

I will invent some new language for this, I thought.

Look, the post van remembers its primitive dance. Likewise the flashing train.

Some things are difficult to understand: Ireland, Zoroastrianism, geophagy, plasma physics. But in fact they can be understood, as well as participated in.

I was so happy in my breathing there. I did not need to keep waking belief up, from its drugged sleep.

(When I was dying, it was my mother's job, every few hours, or several times an hour, to wake me. She shook me slightly, insistently, by the shoulder or the arm. She called my name.) (And I said, later, yes, belief is like that.)

[CARREGLWYD)

Gift. You really could shed your blood here, if you wanted to. (Who would know.) Every mammal-sign, plunging downward.

I sort my breaths into three piles, one red, one short, one kind.

Repeat the collect of nettles, from memory. Memory's apsed plantation, its shelter-belt.

Having never been "lost" in the forest as a child, merely at times not knowing my relation to other beings.

Palanquin of the language arts, this is a conifer. This, on the stone, is fresh blood.

I lift you to the stile, inheritor. Blackened masque threading the vow with its distaff lambs.

Everything is broken, the land included. Somehow I feel reassured by this.

Burnt folds casting their opal shadows, their sleeping ewes. The archers, resting their bow-arms.

I want the wind's debt to climb my banquet plate, I want tons of perfect glass. I check my arms for scars: they're all still there.

Let's frighten the lambs again, whispers gravity. Let's blind their faith in safety.

If my child dies, I won't be the one leaving toys on her grave, the woman in the coffee shop said, to her friend.

Who, then. Constellations of indulgences, this or that many repetitions, this or that many years.

By which I mean: *Gift.* It knocks the spirit right out of you, & into someone else.

Residue of autoharp, of zither, childhood's insatiable paranoias. I watched the town "take shape," as they say, in the valley below.

And here again is our friend the verb *to glisten.*

Gift. The clock's softest, inmost organs; the breath's gilt frame. Cry of the herdsman at the farmstead, cries of the herdsmen in the plain.

[LLANDYFEISANT CHURCH (II)]

There are worse temporary fates, the saints advise. Zion is a
   wheel, is what the clouds say.
What can a wheel know. A bit of litter at the curb, a broken arch.
Yesterday I crossed the same field of freshly-mown hay four times.
   I was sweating, I was anxious.
I had learned to breathe again, just hours before.
What then is the purpose of saints. (Companions; goads. My
   friend visits the wildlife refuge for similar purposes.)
Distant playground shouts of the children at recess; birdcalls I
   can't decipher.
You know you carry it with you.
Observe the wheel, the evolution of spokes, rotation's skeleton.
   Observe the ivy, its vertical obeisance.
I sang the hymn as I'd been taught it, not as it appeared in the
   red book.
The exact footprint, the guidebook specified. I compare the foot,
   to the wheel. (O Zion.)
It's not a poem if it doesn't have a gun in it, or at least the threat
   of a gun in it, my friend claimed. We were on our way to the
   auditions.
And our other friend, our mutual friend, packing house again,
   planning a new home on the other side of that large
   continent.
Owls active in daylight hours. The respiration of lichens, both
   before & after heavy rain.
It's true, I wish we didn't have to speak. Or, that we had not spoken.
The axle, fitted to the wheel, its transverse spoke.
Inside, cool darkness. Is this "disused" enough. Refuse of the failed
   visitor's center, & of the wealthy dead.
Somehow I am always cast in the role of minor villain, i.e. though

I do calculable harm, nothing changes because of me.

Not the dog-rose. Not the saints' tongues, curing on their splintered board. Not the five-lobed campion, nor the foxglove, that the bees worship. (And the flies.)

I sit in the most abandoned seats, because there is safety in desolation. I pat down my blood, as if for spare change.

The wheel has all the speaking parts, & that's fine, really.

I apprenticed myself to ghosts. The animals approach, then back away. Once again, I'm blocking their route to the water.

The last of the dead have processioned out of our lives; the first of the living arrive. (The *fists* of the living, I almost wrote.)

When the visitor's center was no longer deemed safe for children, it was closed.

Let's store our spare barbed wire here, someone suggested; let's polish the wheel. —But there is no wheel here, master. (And likewise no master.)

Vines dangle from the rafters. The useless track lighting.

Imagine what the living once did, the saints murmur, vaguely accusatory. Not just here; anywhere.

So I do. Because it is not a wheel of the dead, but a wheel of the living (etc. etc.).

The well lies just outside the door, heavy with padlocks, justified. The campion, the nettle. The jackdaw I spoke to, all creaturely for a moment, forgetting.

Because only man forgets. (O my indemnities, O my chevalier.)

You should have drawn a clearer diagram, you told me. —True enough. I have always been terrible at drawing.

Promise me something. What. Anything.

That when we live here again, we will not be monsters. Or, being monsters, that we will sleep, that we will find rest, our separate rests.

That what we bring in will be what we bear out. Due honor to matter.

The dust of all things, trellised. The return of languages, from

114

those who have handled them.

For we too know wheels, & are known of them.

Perfect, as that Christ of the trades surrounded by tools, tools & their material shadows. Alongside some music we had made. Or just after.

NOTES ON POEMS

Many of the references in the poems are glossed in the poems themselves. A few additional notes:

"American Goshawk": Written at the MacDowell Colony in Peterborough, New Hampshire. Technically it is a *North* American goshawk.

"Caynham Camp": a well-preserved Iron Age hill fort southeast of Ludlow, in Herefordshire.

"Mutter Museum with Owl": in Philadelphia. The "friend" in the poem is Brian Teare, who accompanied me there.

"North Walsham": in Norfolk. The "famous writer" was Agatha Christie. The tiny parish church at Edingthorpe, where Sassoon spent part of his childhood, is a few miles to the east. Doggerland is a modern name for the vast country further east that once connected Britain to continental Europe and disappeared beneath the sea after the last ice age thaw.

"Broken Things": Morwenstow, Cornwall, was the seat of the Victorian antiquarian and poet Rev. R. S. Hawker, in whose former rectory I was permitted to stay. His writing studio was built into the side of a nearby cliff using scavenged timbers from shipwrecks.

"Never-Ending Bells": the title borrows from a stray line of Michaux, in translation. "Peeping Tom" is the local nickname for the medieval church tower at Hartland, Devon, which due to vagaries of topography often seems to sneak up in the landscape, at surprising distances.

"In Him Were Hidden All Our Tongues": the title is drawn from a line of St Ephrem the Syrian, again in translation. Cliffside was a textile mill village (company town) in Rutherford County, North Carolina. Most Southern textile mills exited the housing market between 1935 and 1960, selling to their employee-occupants (who were sometimes forced to buy). The company that owned Cliffside and neighboring Avondale preferred to demolish the villages: everything except the few buildings that either were owned by others on ground leased from the company (at Cliffside, two churches and the post office) or were located just off company property (the school). The mills continued to operate for a few decades before they closed and were in turn demolished. The Church of the Exceptional ("For the Physically & Mentally Handicapped" as per signage) was at the time of writing just up the road from Cliffside and Avondale, on the outskirts of the former mill village of Henrietta.

"Blue Heron, Marlborough": Marlborough, New Hampshire. The Pioneer Valley Sacred Harp Singing is held annually in Sunderland, Massachusetts. The Carl Carmer reference is to his (much older) account of a Sacred Harp singing in *Stars Fell on Alabama*.

"Only Coerce Yourself Gently, & Show": a mushroom-hunting poem, in honor of Peter O'Leary. The title comes from a stray line (in translation) of the 6th-century Syrian mystic Dadisho'.

"Wordwell" triptych: the abandoned early Norman church at Wordwell, West Suffolk, on the site of a deserted medieval village and at the edge of the King's Forest, is noted for its examples of early stone carving that have thus far resisted conclusive interpretation.

"On Hearing a Cuckoo at Pentecost": Lackford, West Suffolk, or more precisely the ancient track between Lackford and Risby.

"West Stow Orchard" poems: the small orchard at West Stow Hall, West Suffolk, where I was in fact a (paying) guest for a week in 2018.

"St Melangell's Day, Eastnor": Melangell was one of that great concourse of poorly-documented 5th- and 6th-century Welsh saints; her legend includes the story of a hare that hid itself in her skirts whilst in flight from the hunting party of a Welsh prince. The "dim town" of the poem is Ledbury, known somewhat for a much later recluse, Katherine de Audley. The Eastnor poems were all drafted on the Eastnor estate, southeast of Ledbury.

"[Additional Eastnor Poem (IX)]": Ernst Chladni (1756-1827), musician and physicist, often known as the "father of acoustics," who pioneered the classification of vibrations by recording the patterns made by vibrating dust on rigid membranes.

"The Earliest Witnesses": "What is permanent / versus what is splendor" refers to Michael Palmer's poem "Echo," in *Codes Appearing*, p. 132.

"Hansen's Disease": the preferred modern term for leprosy. During the writing of parts of this book, as well as its predecessor, I suffered from a neurological condition that for several years resisted diagnosis or treatment. It seemed to be on the Parkinsonian spectrum, but at one point the possibility of Hansen's was floated (ironically, it seemed to me, at the time).

"[Llandyfeisant Church (I)]": a tiny abandoned church of early origin on the Dinefwr estate near Llandeilo, Carmarthenshire. Thanks to Rebecca Killa and Welsh Wildlife for permitting access. Castle Woods and the ruins of Dinefwr Castle are nearby, Dryslwyn a short distance to the west. The Festival of the Senses is an actual event, held annually in Llandeilo, although it sounds like something I would invent, would like to have invented, for the sake of the poem. Because wouldn't you want to go? (—We're already there.)

"[Carn Goch]": an ancient, and huge, Iron Age hillfort four miles northeast of Llandeilo.

"[Carreglwyd]": this particular Carreglwyd is an abandoned farmstead a bit to Carn Goch's south. I am indebted to Peter Larkin's conceptualization of both scarcity and gift.

"[Llandyfeisant Church (II)]": the "Christ of the Trades"—a representation of the crucified Jesus surrounded by medieval hand tools—was an occasional subject of parish church wall paintings in medieval Britain. Some modern accounts explain the image as meant to communicate the lordship of Christ over all human endeavor; others claim it was a morality lesson, implying the harm done to Christ by those who violated the Sabbath by working on Sundays.

Apologies to the sexton (at St Mary's, Eastnor) and the gardener (at Llandyfeisant church), both of whom I accidentally startled, and to patrons of the Mattress Factory Art Museum, same.

ACKNOWLEDGMENTS

The author gratefully acknowledges prior publication of poems in *American Poetry Review, Paris Review, Poetry, Iowa Review, PN Review, Bennington Review, Harvard Review, Kenyon Review, Gulf Coast, Poetry International, Mississippi Review, Image, Copper Nickel, Reliquiae, Cambridge Literary Review, New American Writing, Shearsman, Crazyhorse,* and *Plume.*

Warm thanks to Andy & Eileen Gilbert of West Stow Hall; to the Eastnor Castle estate; to Jill Welby in Morwenstow; and to Bucknell University for funding that enabled me to travel to these places.

Thank you, Lannan Foundation and MacDowell Colony. Best of thanks to friends who read poems from this collection and held the lamp: Ilya Kaminsky, Tim Lilburn, Dana Levin, John Gallaher, Peter O'Leary, Shane McCrae, Karla Kelsey, Victoria Chang, John Lane, and Rachel Galvin.

CPSIA information can be obtained
at www.ICGtesting.com
Printed in the USA
LVHW032235030722
722684LV00004B/451

9 781946 482488